A New Dawn for Christianity

A New Dawn for Christianity

Embracing an Honest Christian Paradigm

Barry E. Blood Sr.
Rev. Michael MacMillan

Library of Congress Control Number: 2017919706
CreateSpace Independent Publishing Platform, North Charleston, SC

If the river of our Christian story is not flowing, we will cease to be, for we will cease to be in tune with the very nature of the universe, forever seeking new form, forever unfolding into what has never been known before. Just as in sleep every night we descend into the unconscious to be renewed, so our Christian story needs to reenter the world of dreaming and imagining to be born anew.

—John Phillip Newell, *The Rebirthing of God*

Acknowledgements

We would be remiss if we did not give special recognition to Mrs. Betsy Riebsomer Draper, Mr. Paul Draper, Dr. Wendy Brand and Mr. Jonathan Perera for their dedicated effort in assisting with the information, review and editing of this book. From rough draft through final manuscript their professional guidance, and critical assessment added immeasurably to the quality of the finished product.

Contents

Acknowledgments   vii
Preface   xi
1 The Thanksgiving Visit   1
2 Profound New Knowledge   8
3 Second Guessing   16
4 The Concept of God   20
5 Seeking Validation   31
6 Shocking Revelation   38
7 The Savior Motif   45
8 More Confirmation   55
9 The Word of God   61
10 The Accident   67
11 To Whom Shall We Pray?   71
12 Getting on With Life   77
13 Original Sin and Atonement   88
14 The Trinity   99
15 The Struggle   108
16 The Second Coming and Life After Death   112
17 The Synoptic Gospels   119
18 Final Session   134
19 Progressive Sermons   149
    Introduction   149
    What is Progressive Christianity?   160
    What is This Thing Called God? - Part One 168
    What is This Thing Called God? - Part Two 176
    The Bible   184
    Knockdown in Nicaea - The Trinity   191
    From Galilee to God: An Honest Image of Jesus 199
    Death and the Afterlife   206
    Prayer   213
20 Study Group Ideas   221
21 Afterword   229
Notes   232
Bibliography   235

Preface

The ability to acquire, retain, assimilate, process, and use information is one of the mental attributes that differentiates human beings from other animal species. Humans have always displayed a thirst for knowledge and throughout history have striven to add to and increase their knowledge, in every field of human endeavor.

From the earliest records of human existence, mankind's knowledge has increased with each succeeding generation. Knowledge builds upon knowledge. What we know today, becomes the foundation for what we will know tomorrow, and what we will know tomorrow will certainly be subjected to scrutiny in the days and years beyond.

We can envision this expansion of knowledge by critiquing a couple of obvious areas of modern life. For example: It was not much more than a hundred years ago that man's only means of freeing himself from the bonds of gravity was the hot air balloon. Today most of us have experienced the thrill of flying in a jetliner. We can travel across the country, or around the world, in a matter of hours. At this very moment there are astronauts aboard an international space laboratory orbiting the earth at a rate of once every ninety minutes, and we accept it pretty much as matter-of-fact. And who knows what the future has in store for us in the world of aviation? Our continued growth in knowledge has made this phenomenon possible.

Or consider the world of communications. In today's age of computerization, most of us communicate via the Internet, and cell phones. However, only 150 years ago the Pony Express was the premier means of communication.

We needn't even begin to mention the advances in medicine, the sciences and technology. And we can be fairly confident that what we know today, in any of these fields, will be outdated a hundred years from now.

All of us benefit directly or indirectly from this continued explosion of knowledge. We might yearn from time to time for "the good ole' days", but when one stops and really thinks of the conveniences in our lives today brought about by advances of knowledge in every field of endeavor, it's really hard to think about "the good ole' days" as . . . well, . . . "the good ole' days!"

Most of us are willing participants in this explosion of knowledge whether it is in our vocation or hobbies. Just stop and think of the expertise or knowledge you posses in a given field, as an engineer, or as a store manager, or as a homemaker, as a cake decorator, doctor, lawyer, merchant, or teacher.

As a society we place a high value on current, up-to-date knowledge in every field. Every field, that is, *except religion*. When it comes to religion we seem to want to believe that our ancient ancestors knew all there was to know about things religious, and no new knowledge can ever improve upon that ancient knowledge.

Somehow, vast numbers of Christians have convinced themselves that the unknown writers who wrote the Bible, (between 950 BCE and 125 CE), possessed the ultimate knowledge of the universe and its workings for all time. They believe that the writers were somehow "inspired" by a supernatural being, the supreme creator of the universe, and have somehow convinced themselves that no new religious knowledge has been discovered in the ensuing three thousand years. Others recognize that there have been new discoveries but feel they must be suppressed lest they cause confusion and perhaps do damage to the earlier beliefs.

Three thousand years ago, the religious knowledge of the day was written down in documents that are today known as the Old and New Testaments. At the time they were written, these documents contained the most current, the most profound knowledge of religion known to the Jewish world. The documents contain that ancient understanding of God, the universe, the workings of nature, and mankind's role in the world. The teachings of the Christian and Jewish religions are, even today, based on these documents.

However, in the ensuing three thousand years, much new knowledge *has obviously* been gathered in these areas, knowledge that supersedes, updates, adds to, and corrects the knowledge of those who wrote the Old and New Testaments.

Much of this new information is exciting, enlightening and liberating. Most of this new knowledge is known to the clergy of the church, *yet it remains hidden from the laity, the people in the pews.*

The question to be asked is this; Why has the Church been so reluctant to teach the people in the pews, about what they themselves know to be true? Knowledge that is taught in the seminaries, but in most instances, not spoken from the pulpit. In fact, most of what is spoken or implied from the pulpit, from Sunday to Sunday, is in direct conflict with what is taught in most reputable seminaries. The result of this inaction: *While every other area of human endeavor has moved forward with new knowledge and understanding, our religious teachings remain mired in the worldview of our ancient past.*

If Christianity is to survive in the twenty-first century, it must embrace and build upon the knowledge and worldview of today, and relegate the doctrine of the past to the annals of history and ancient experience.

If the Church is to be a part of the intellect of today's society, it must preach the doctrine of the past as the human experience that *was*, not the human experience that *is*. Failing to do so, will, in the not too distant future, relegate the Church to the fringes of society among the uneducated and the uninformed. National polls and surveys continue to show that this trend is, unfortunately, already happening.

The Church, and the people in the pews, must not fear new knowledge. Knowledge is power. Knowledge is the tool we human beings use to navigate the wilderness of life.

Chapters One through Eighteen of this book are intended to help close the knowledge gap that exists between "popular" Christianity, or the doctrine as it is preached from the pulpit and "academic" Christianity, meaning the doctrine as it is taught in reputable colleges and seminaries. These chapters are presented in a 'narrative nonfiction' genre.

The story line of this section revolves around a fictionalized group of students studying Christianity at the university level. The dialogue between the students and their professor allows for discussion of controversial issues in a sensitive, educational setting. The students become the voice and thoughts of the reader as they question the validity of doctrinal differences between what they have been taught in Sunday school and church, and what the professor is teaching them.

Perhaps you, the reader, will identify with the angst and trepidation of the students as they attempt to deal with this new information.

Please keep in mind, the information imparted to the students by Prof. Tracy is current Christian scholarship. Likewise, the information contained in the conversations between Greg Chambers and Rev. Hill and Rev. Fulling is also based on today's information.

Chapters Nineteen and Twenty are written with the local pastor or study group in mind. So often we hear stories of clergy wanting to introduce their congregation to modern interpretations of doctrine that they were taught in seminary but are reluctant to do so for fear of jeopardizing their jobs. (Further discussion on this situation may be found in Chapter 14) Pastors are usually not given much, if any, instruction on how to introduce new Christian knowledge during their academic studies.

We have attempted to provide sermons and study group ideas that will help educate and inform pastors and congregations in a non-threatening way.

We hope you will read with an open mind, understanding that although this information may be new to you, *it has been known to Christian scholars for more than 200 years!*

BEB MM

1

The Thanksgiving Visit

Life is good!
A light autumn breeze caused the red and orange leaves to swirl and dance as if they were alive. Greg and Lea sat near the cafeteria window, enjoying the view. Saturday mornings were the only time in their hectic week that permitted such leisure.

Lea Wong, a student from Beijing, China and Gregory Chambers, born and raised in a small town in southern Indiana, were as different as night and day in every way one might think, yet they had forged a friendship from the very day they were paired in freshman chemistry class. Now, in their second year at Bradley University in Peoria, Illinois, the friendship continued, but it was still more of a "brother/sister" relationship than anything else.

Greg had been toying with the idea of asking Lea if she would like to go home with him over the upcoming Thanksgiving holidays. He knew she would not be going home to China and, well . . . maybe she would enjoy meeting his family and getting away from the campus for a few days. Still he worried about how to ask her, for fear she would get the wrong idea. The only time they had ever spent together outside the classroom was to study in the library or to have lunch in the cafeteria. There was the one time they sat together at a basketball game, but they were with several other friends.

"School has only been in session five weeks," said Greg, "but it seems like it's been five months."

"Yeah," replied Lea, "I think it has to do with the fact that our classes are so much harder this year."

"You can say that again," quipped Greg.

"Well, anyway, we've got some time off coming up soon . . . Thanksgiving will be here in a few weeks . . .You got any plans?" he asked.

"Not really. Nancy is staying on campus too, so we'll probably do something together. She has a car, you know. She said something about maybe driving up to Chicago for a couple days."

"Oh," said Greg, and dropped the subject.

—)(—

Sunday morning, as usual, Greg made his way to the little Methodist church a few blocks north of the campus. He had always gone to church as a child and teen, so when he started college it was natural for him to continue the ritual. That, and the fact that his mother had insisted he do so. In his hometown of Princeton, he had been a member of the youth group at the First United Methodist Church. He enjoyed the friendship of the group and the involvement with the church. His family—mom, dad and younger sister Becky— were not overly religious. They attended Sunday school and church most Sunday mornings, he and Becky went to youth group, and they obediently said grace at meal time, but that was about the extent of their religious life. Still, Greg considered himself a religious person.

The sermon this morning was on "Living every day for the Lord". The routine was always the same: welcome, sing a hymn, prayer, sing another hymn, read the scripture, prayer, pass the offering plate, sing the Doxology, listen to the sermon, sing another hymn, pronounce the benediction, everybody out. Yes, it was a familiar routine, but it was also comforting and grounding for a young man, away from his family and his boyhood surroundings.

After church Greg headed back to his room in a private home just a couple blocks from the campus. He would spend the afternoon and evening reading his English literature assignment, boring, but necessary. As he read, his mind wandered. It was hard to stay focused today for some reason. Maybe it was because the weather was still so pleasantly fall-ish. The warm sunlight was coming through the window, beckoning him to get out and walk in the crisp autumn air.

He began to think again about the Thanksgiving holidays and the idea of having Lea go home with him. "Darn it," he thought, "why didn't I just go ahead and ask her? If she would rather stay here she would say so and that would be that. Tomorrow I'm going to ask her no matter what."

Greg had always been rather shy. Maybe timid would be a better word to use. He knew what he wanted to say, but just couldn't let it out, so to speak. Then later, he would get mad at himself for remaining silent. This had caused him much grief in high school and relegated him to the role of a loner. A likable and friendly guy, but all the same, a loner.

—)(—

It was Tuesday afternoon before Greg saw Lea again. She was walking across the campus toward the library carrying an armload of books and a full backpack. He approached her from behind, tapped her on the shoulder and said jokingly, "Can I help you with those books, Miss?"

Then, before she could hardly turn to acknowledge him, he blurted out, "Would you like to go home with me at Thanksgiving and spend a few days there with me and my family? I think you would like my parents and my sister. And you've really never had a chance to see any of the countryside except around Peoria and we could just bum around for a few days and relax around the house, or whatever. What do you think?"

"Oh, . . . well," began Lea.

"But if you don't want to that's okay," Greg interrupted.

"Well, . . ." she began again.

"If you've already committed to Nancy, I'll understand," he interrupted again.

"Actually, I think it would be fun. I'd like to visit your family," she finally interjected.

Greg paused, then said "Uh, wow that's great! Hey then, we'll have fun, I promise."

He had done it, he had asked her to spend the Thanksgiving holidays with him and his family and she accepted! That was rather easy. He began to feel excited. His parents would pick them up and drive them to Princeton. There would be lots of time to talk and get to really know each other. He would be proud to take her around town and show her where he had spent his childhood. And he was sure his family would like Lea.

—)(—

Thanksgiving was a big deal for the Chambers family. They were truly thankful for the blessings of the comfortable middle class life style they had attained. Leon Chambers, Greg's father, was a supervisor at a local electronics firm and Helen Chambers, Greg's mom, was an elementary teacher.

No other relatives, from either side of the family, lived in the area. So except for the occasional time that a relative was visiting, holiday observances were a very close-knit family affair. Having Lea there would be a very special occasion.

The Friday before Thanksgiving was a bright sunny day. Leon had planned to travel to Peoria alone to pick up Greg and Lea, but Helen decided at the last moment to ride along. It was a pleasant trip; 225 miles each way. They would meet the kids for dinner Friday evening, stay overnight at a local motel, and drive home on Saturday.

—)(—

Greg was somewhat apprehensive about introducing Lea to his parents. He had brought friends home before but never a female friend and never one of such a different culture. But the introductions went well; Mom and Dad were pleased to meet Lea and made her feel comfortable almost at once.

The drive home Saturday was uneventful. Lea was in awe of the vast expanse of farmland that covered central Illinois and southern Indiana. The corn and soybean crops had all been harvested, and many of the fields were already prepared for next season's planting. Driving along in the car one could see flat land for miles and miles in every direction. This was certainly a new experience for Lea.

Seeing Greg's hometown for the first time was an equally awesome experience for her. Having grown up in Beijing, a very populous area of China, and attending school in Peoria, a city of nearly two hundred thousand people, she had never experienced a small town with a population of only eight thousand.

"It looks *liqi youqu*", she said, using the Mandarin word for quaint.

In typical Midwest fashion, Princeton was built with a huge majestic courthouse right in the center of the town. It was a beautiful building of red brick and white limestone trim, built in 1884. High in the belfry was a clock with a bell that chimed the hour of the day and the warm sound was a reassuring resonance for the residents of this little municipality.

Leon Chambers drove a few blocks north of the square to the family home and parked in the driveway. Greg jumped out and rushed around the car to open the door for Lea. He would be the gentleman, hoping to make her feel comfortable in a strange place.

Greg's sixteen year old sister, Becky, showed Lea to the guest room while Helen set about preparing dinner. Greg put his things in his room and made his way to the kitchen. "So mom, what do you think of Lea?" he asked.

"Oh, she certainly is a nice young lady. Do you have any classes with her this year?"

"No, but we see each other every few days, around campus." he replied.

"Well, just don't let things get too serious, after all you still have a lot of schooling ahead of you."

"Mom, we're just friends."

After dinner Greg asked his father for the keys to the car. He wanted to show Lea around town. They drove back to the square. He pointed out Greek's soda shop and candy store where he had worked during high school. Then it was off to Winkler's drive-in restaurant in the South end of town. Greg reminisced about the great breaded tenderloin sandwiches they made there, but since they had just finished eating dinner, the proof of his statement would have to wait for another time.

On their way back to the North end of town, Greg swung by the Methodist church where he had spent so much time in his younger years. The current structure had been built in 1896, a beautiful red brick building with huge stained glass windows on three sides. Greg knew his way around the inside of the old church like the back of his hand. He probably knew of little nooks and crannies the custodian wasn't even aware of. As a member of the Boy Scout troop and the Youth Group, Greg had played hide-and-seek games in every corner of the building, from top to bottom. Lea was impressed with the beauty of the church. Greg explained that they would be attending services there tomorrow morning and she would get to see the grandeur of the inside.

On Sunday morning Lea was impressed with the huge pipe organ, the sound of which seemed to make every wall in the church vibrate. The sun shining through the stained glass windows caused a rainbow of colors to dance across the entire expanse of the sanctuary. People moved about greeting one another, shaking hands, waving to each other across the pews. It seemed to be such a friendly place, not at all like the subdued atmosphere of the Buddhist temple she was used to in her homeland.

Once the service began, Lea was all eyes and ears, taking in every sight and sound. For Greg it was Sunday as usual. The feeling of familiarity made him feel warm all over. He was home.

Driving back home, after the service, Lea was full of questions. She had been intrigued by the various elements of the Christian worship service. She asked Greg about the prayers, the hymns, she asked about God, the Trinity, and the Son of God. The scripture reading had been about Jesus walking on the water and this too puzzled her.

Greg was glad she had enjoyed the service, but at the same

time, he felt inadequate trying to answer some of her questions.

"Let me think about it for a while. Right now I'm too hungry to concentrate!" he said.

—)(—

The balance of their time in Princeton was very relaxed. It was good not to have to be running from class to class, reading and preparing for tests. They slipped away from the house at lunch time one day and drove back to Winkler's drive-in to feast on one of the breaded pork tenderloins Greg had bragged about. Lea had certainly not eaten anything like it in Beijing.

For the next hour or so they just drove around, enjoying the scenery. They drove out the old Petersburg road and looked at the lovely homes. They traveled east of town toward Camp Carson where Greg had spent several summers of his youth, then west of town toward the Wabash River. It was a beautiful fall afternoon and they lost themselves in the moment.

2

Profound New Knowledge

Back in Peoria, it was time to open the books again. It seemed they had been away for a month, though it had only been a week and Greg's brain seemed to have a hard time getting back in gear. He struggled to remember the assignment for his Sociology class. Was it Chapters 6 and 7, or 8 and 9? Had he completed his American History paper or not? In a fog, he stumbled out of the shower and began to gather his wits.

Lea, on the other hand, was having no problem at all getting back in the swing of things. She had called her friend Maria and arranged to meet her for breakfast.

"It was so much fun," said Lea, "and I really liked his parents. They were really nice."

"What was their home like?" asked Maria.

"Well, it was a lot like the homes you see here in Peoria," replied Lea. "Only the whole town seemed more, . . . I don't know, relaxed or something."

"Hmm, well I'm glad you had a good time. It was certainly boring around here."

The door of the small cafe opened and Greg entered. "Over here Greg, come sit with us," called Lea.

"Hey, what are you guys up to?"

"Just talkin'," replied Maria, "Sounds like you two had a good time over Thanksgiving break. I want to go with you next time!"

"Sure, why not, the more the merrier." quipped Greg

"You know, Greg," began Lea, "you still owe me that talk

about your religion. You said you would explain some things to me."

"Yeah, well, I'm not sure I know enough about it myself, I mean, you know, to explain it to you in an intelligent way."

"What's that about?" asked Maria.

"We went to Greg's church last Sunday and I was intrigued by all the stuff I heard. Greg said he would explain it to me, but now it sounds like he wants to chicken out!"

"Wait a minute now," Greg laughed, "I said I'd think about it. I'm not a preacher you know."

"Sure, but you ought to know enough to explain it to someone." returned Lea.

"Hey, you know what," said Maria, "I gotta go, but I know a guy that might be able to explain church stuff to you. He used to teach a religion course, and now he teaches philosophy. I've got his class on Friday mornings. His name is Prof. Tracy."

"Maybe we'll stop by his office," Lea said.

"You really mean that?" asked Greg.

"Sure," replied Lea, "Why not? Maybe he can teach you something too."

Greg wasn't real excited about asking Prof. Tracy, a stranger, to explain Christianity to Lea, but he had to admit, it would be easier than trying to do it himself.

—)(—

The sign above the door said Dr. Andrew Tracy, PhD. Greg knocked and a voice inside said, "Come in!"

After introducing themselves, Lea explained their reason for being there."Well," said Andrew Tracy, "I haven't taught a class in religion for six years, and I'm not scheduled to teach one any time in the near future. But if it's just a bit of an introduction to Christianity that you want, why don't you just go to a local church and talk to the pastor?"

"I guess we could do that, but a friend brought up your name, so we thought. . . ."

"Tell you what I'll do." said Prof. Tracy. "If you can get a few more of your friends interested, maybe six or so, I'll conduct a short eight or nine week course for you that will explain more about Christianity than you ever wanted to know."

"Wow!" exclaimed Lea, "You'd do that for us?"

"Well, I kinda miss teaching religion so this would be sort of a treat for me too. But understand, what I will offer you will not be the pabulum that you are used to getting in Sunday school."

Greg and Lea looked at each other quizzically. "I don't understand," remarked Greg.

"I will only do this if you are interested in learning about Christianity at the academic level. I don't have any desire to feed you a bunch of 'once upon a time' stories, as if you are a group of six year olds."

Greg answered, "Okay, I guess," not at all knowing exactly what he was agreeing to.

"Okay then," said Prof. Tracy, "See if you can round up a few others and if you can meet me here next Wednesday evening at 7. That is the only evening I have open."

"Thank you Prof. Tracy, we'll be here!" said Lea excitedly.

Greg and Lea had enough friends on campus that they didn't have any trouble finding several who were willing to participate in their ad hoc class. Lea enlisted her friend Maria and two others, Sandra and Helen, from her Ethics class. Greg brought along Ted and Jon from his sociology class. Then there were two others, Carol and Vince from the young adult class at the Methodist church that Greg attended.

—)(—

Lea was excited, but Greg was apprehensive. He was still wondering what Prof. Tracy meant when he said he wasn't interested in teaching them "once upon a time" stories. Well, he guessed he would find out soon enough. He was just a block away from Prof. Tracy's office when Lea's path intersected his.

"Hi, are we going to be on time?" questioned Lea.

"Yeah," replied Greg, "We've still got ten minutes."

They walked in silence. The air was chilly, and the leaves rustled under their feet. They could see some of the others gathered at the entrance of Westlake Hall where Prof. Tracy had his office.

Andrew Tracy had been a Professor at Bradley for eighteen years. He had taught religion for the first twelve years of his career, but when an opening had occurred in the philosophy department he decided to change fields. "Actually," he would say, "religion and philosophy are closely related."

When they entered the office, Prof. Tracy stood and announced, "I have reserved the small conference room just two doors down the hall to the right. It will give us a little more space."

As they turned and made their way out into the hall, the rest of the invited friends joined them. Greg was amazed at how punctual everyone had been, especially Ted who was late to almost every class he ever attended.

After a quick round of introductions, Prof. Tracy spoke. "Let's start with a bit of informal conversation about why we are here. I know that Mr. Chambers and Ms Wong are here because Ms Wong is interested in learning about the Christian religion. Why are the rest of you here?"

Silence and blank stares filled the room. After a brief pause, Maria Sanchez spoke, "Well, I'm here, basically because Lea ask me to come."

Several others around the table nodded in agreement.

"But I also want to get a better understanding of some of the Christian stuff." added Jon Parker, a third year chemistry major.

"Yeah," exclaimed Vince Morgan, "There is so much mystery to the things in the Bible. It would be nice to understand some of that stuff better."

"Are all of you, except for Ms Wong, Christians?" asked Prof. Tracy.

All nodded affirmatively. "But I would have to say, I haven't been inside a church since I was about six years old." added Ted Wallace."

"Why is that?" asked Prof. Tracy.

"Well, mom and dad divorced and I lived with mom and she worked so hard all week she just wanted to crash on Sunday, I guess. I went to the youth group at the Baptist church a couple times, but never really got interested in it."

"I guess I'm just the opposite of Ted," said Carol Burke. "I've attended the Methodist church, actually Sunday school, church, and youth group, almost every Sunday since I can remember."

"Anyone grow up in the Catholic church?" Prof. Tracy inquired.

"I did," answered Sandra Taylor.

"So did I," said Helen Fredrick, "But I switched to the Baptist church about two years ago."

"Why did you do that?" quizzed Prof. Tracy.

"I don't know, I guess 'cause some of my best friends went there," Helen replied.

"Did your parents object to your switching?" asked Prof. Tracy.

"No, they had pretty much dropped out of church several years ago. They didn't care." said Helen.

"I've always been a Presbyterian," said Maria. "And I attend Sunday school and worship service every Sunday."

"Okay, let me see if I can summarize what we have here," said Prof. Tracy. "Mr. Chambers and Ms Wong are here so Ms Wong can learn about Christianity. The rest of you are sort of here because your friends asked you to come along and a few of you think you might learn something of interest, and that's about it. Does that about sum it up?"

Everyone nodded in agreement.

"Now, let me tell you what I am willing to do. You see, I taught religion for several years and enjoyed it very much. My students were mostly young men and women who were preparing for the ministry. I taught history of religion in general, history of Christianity, and the origins of Christian doctrine. Good stuff, important stuff if you are going to be an educated church leader. Or so I thought." Prof. Tracy paused for just a second.

"What do you mean, 'or so you thought'?" asked Lea.

"Well, after pouring several years of teaching effort into the process, I discovered that when most of my students made their way back into the real world and into the pulpit of a church somewhere, they simply preached and taught the same things they had been taught in Sunday school since infancy. It was as if nothing I had taught them had sunk in."

"Wait, are you saying that, what they learned from Sunday school is somehow different than what you taught them?" questioned Jon Parker.

"Exactly," said Prof. Tracy. "And what I propose to teach you are the same things I taught my students, the same information that is taught in every reputable college or seminary in the country. Factual information about the history of Christianity, religion, and Christian doctrine. Make no mistake about it, it will shock some of you. It will cause some of you to become very upset with me and possibly leave the group, but those who stay will learn a great deal that will serve them well for the rest of their life. Now, with that being said, who is in and who is out?"

"But . . . are you saying that somehow what you're going to explain to us isn't what we've been told by our churches?" asked Ted.

"Mr. Wallace, there are two levels of understanding in the Christian religion. One is called Popular Christianity, which is what one hears from the pulpit every Sunday morning, and the other is called Academic Christianity. Academic Christianity is what is taught in most seminaries and colleges the world over. Usually it is not preached from the pulpit. It should be, but it isn't. It is as if there is an invisible velvet curtain hanging between the pulpit and the pews. A curtain that separates the people from the pastor or priest and it separates Popular Christianity from Academic Christianity."

"But why?" asked Sandra.

"Well, there are a couple of reasons, Ms Taylor," continued Prof. Tracy, "But we're not going to get into that area of discussion this evening. That will come in due time."

He continued, "I'm getting a little bit ahead of where I wanted to be in this first discussion, but maybe some of this will help you understand better what we will be discussing later if you stay."

"Well, I know I'm staying," said Ted, "You've piqued my curiosity—I gotta hear more!"

Several others agreed.

Greg, on the other hand, remained silent. He was a bit skeptical of what Prof. Tracy was saying. Still, it would be hard for him to back out now since he was co-instigator of the group in the first place. He would keep quiet and listen. Maybe he was misunderstanding what Prof. Tracy was saying.

"Okay then," said Prof. Tracy, "Let's begin to begin. So that you have a good understanding of what will come later, we are going to begin our adventure some thirty thousand years ago. That is the time period that history reflects the beginnings of man's journey with gods and goddesses. It was about this time that humans had developed enough cognitive thinking power to be able to observe and question the world around them."

Raising her hand, Helen said, "The Baptist church where I go says that God formed the earth about six thousand years ago. Why is that?"

"Some religions believe they can determine the age of the earth by tracing certain genealogy scriptures that appear in the Bible," replied Prof. Tracy, "Scientific knowledge has disproved that idea over and over again, just as it has shown that the earth is not flat. Yet, there are those who claim the Bible is completely true and without error and so they still believe that the earth is only six or eight thousand years old. I've got socks that are older than that, but that won't change some people's mind either!"

Everyone chuckled.

"Helen, many of the things I will explain to you in these classes will go against the popular teachings of the Baptists and other denominations. It's not that the hierarchy of the church doesn't know better, it's just that they don't preach what they know to be true. That gets into the subject of Popular vs. Academic religion that I mentioned earlier. We'll talk more about that later. Just know for now that what I will be telling you is based on history, archaeology, anthropology, geology, and many other fields of science, and is backed by scientific evidence. In some areas it will support the Bible and in others it will not. In the end, I think you will have a much clearer picture of Christianity, and that's what I think you all agree is why you are here."

Everyone nodded, though Greg was still a bit apprehensive.

"Prof. Tracy, you said humans have been around for thirty thousand years. " said Jon, "I thought they had been around much longer than that."

"What I said was, that's when humans acquired the rudiments of cognitive thinking and began asking questions and seeking answers to the wonders of nature around them." replied Prof. Tracy.

"So, is that when humans started thinking about God?" asked Jon.

Prof. Tracy sat back in his chair and assessed the expressions on the faces around the table. They were all staring at him, waiting for his response. He had never done an abbreviated class such as this and if he continued on this subject it would bring up the issue of God much sooner than he would have preferred. He would rather have had a chance to get to know the members of the group a bit better before arriving at this point in the class. Nevertheless, here it was, ready or not!

Before anyone could speak, Prof. Tracy said, "We'll explore the answer to that question when we meet next week. You can consider that to be your homework for the week. Give it some thought, do some reading, and see what you can discover. The question is, 'When did humans start thinking about God?'"

3

Second Guessing

The temperature had dropped significantly while they were in their meeting with Prof. Tracy. Now, as they left Westlake Hall, they felt the sting of the wind on their faces.

"Who's up for a cup of coffee?" asked Jon.

"Sounds good, but I need to get back to the dorm and study." said Sandra.

"Me too," replied Carol.

"Well, the library cafe is open for another forty-five minutes, I'm going in." said Jon.

The rest of the group followed him. The Cullom-Davis Library was just next door to Westlake Hall.

Once everyone was seated Ted asked, "So, what did you guys think of the class intro?"

"I didn't get much of an idea of what the class is going to be about," said Maria.

"What?" exclaimed Vince, "I thought he was very explicit."

"Really?" replied Maria. "Then tell me what I missed."

"He said quite clearly that he would teach us the differences between what the people in the pews understand about Christianity and what is taught to the pastors about Christianity. I thought that came over pretty clear," Vince stated.

"Yeah, but what's that got to do with learning about Christianity? That's what I thought we were here for," chided Maria.

"Sounds to me like we're going to get more than we came for," said Lea. "I think Prof. Tracy calls what we came looking for 'Popular Christianity' and he's going to teach us that plus something he calls 'Academic Christianity'."

"Right," said Vince. "Sorta like a two for one deal!"

"Anybody have any ideas about the question he posed, 'When did humans start thinking about God?'" asked Ted.

"I just googled it and there is scads of information on the origin of gods," said Helen. "Looks like the biggest problem will be deciding which sources to believe."

"That's usually the way it is with anything you look up on the net," noted Jon.

"Well," continued Ted, "I know everybody has a busy schedule, even before we start to add this class, but let's all try to check out a few sites in the next few days and maybe try to get back together this weekend to compare notes. What do you think?"

"How about right here, 2:00, Sunday afternoon, anybody who can make it?" suggested Helen.

Everybody agreed to try to meet Sunday afternoon.

—)(—

Greg and Lea walked together across the campus on their way to their rooms.

"I'm excited!" said Lea, "How about you?"

Greg was somewhat non-committal. "Guess it will be okay, although I'm not sure it's what you really wanted. We might have been better off to just talk to Reverend Fulling at my church."

"No way! This is going to be a great experience for all of us," exclaimed Lea.

"Yeah, but what if we get off into areas that we don't want to talk about?" replied Greg.

"Like what? We said we wanted to learn about Christianity and that's what Prof. Tracy is going to talk about. So what could be the problem?"

"I don't know. I just have this funny feeling. . . ."

—)(—

Prof. Tracy wondered if he had been too eager to take on this impromptu class. Perhaps he was simply fulfilling his own need for expression rather than their need for education. These were not seminary students looking to prepare themselves for future service to the church; they were mostly just young kids, here because of the curiosity of one of their friends.

It had always been Prof. Tracy's manner to speak honestly with his students, even when it meant shattering long-held beliefs. He was convinced that honesty was the best and only policy that made sense when it came to teaching religion. While others might pussy-foot around certain issues, he felt obliged to charge ahead with little or no regard for sensitivity. "Truth is truth, there should be no fault in speaking honestly, especially about religion," he mused.

He knew what he was teaching was what Christian scholars had known for the past two hundred years. He also knew that most clergy were reluctant to speak about much of this information, even in private conversation with congregants. This secretive attitude irked him. Was he about to expose this group of young people to something that they were not prepared for emotionally? He pondered these things as he closed up his office and headed home.

"Intellectual honesty," he thought. "There's nothing wrong with intellectual honesty." This would be an opportunity to interject some of that into the thought process of a group of individuals who might otherwise never be given a chance to mature in their Christian faith.

—)(—

Greg woke Wednesday morning to the sound of the wind swirling outside his bedroom window. Before his feet touched the floor his cell phone was ringing. It was Lea.

"Have you looked out the window yet?"

"Are you kidding, I'm not even awake yet," he grumbled.

"Go look, go look!" Lea said excitedly.

Greg pulled back the blind, "Holy crap! First snow of the season!"

It had snowed during the night. It was still snowing and the whole world appeared to be covered with a blanket of white. Everything looked so clean and bright. Snow coverage this complete was rare where Greg grew up in southern Indiana, but here in Peoria it occurred several times each winter. Greg loved the beauty of the new fallen snow and couldn't wait to get out in it.

"Want to meet up for breakfast?" he asked.

"Sure," replied Lea, "I'll meet you at the library cafeteria in forty-five minutes."

What little traffic there was, was moving slowly since the streets had not yet been cleared. As Greg walked across the campus, the snow crunched under his feet. He liked the sound.

Lea arrived soon after Greg had gotten his coffee and taken a seat.

"Wow, winter sorta came on fast, didn't it?" remarked Lea.

"Yeah," replied Greg, "changes the looks of the whole world. I love it!"

"Do you think it will keep any of the group from coming to the meeting with Prof. Tracy this evening?" asked Lea.

"Oh, I forgot this is Wednesday. Nah, six inches of snow shouldn't stop anybody."

"But it's still snowing," Lea commented.

"Yeah, but it will be fine, you'll see," assured Greg.

4

The Concept of God

Everyone was on time except Maria. She had texted Lea she thought she was coming down with a cold and didn't want to contaminate the group. Prof. Tracy arrived five minutes late, complaining about the icy streets.

"Well," Prof. Tracy asked, "did you all have fun trying to discover when humans started thinking about a deity?"

"Yeah," answered Ted, "but I'm not sure I know any more now than before I started looking!"

"I found tons of stuff on the internet," said Sandra.

"From what I found," replied Carol, "it seems like the search for God didn't really start with a god. There seemed to be other religious things before God."

"Like what?" asked Lea.

"Well, like spirits and totems and other stuff. Maybe you could call them gods, I don't know, but the information I found seemed different," added Carol.

"Let me see if I can help you sort this out. I'm sure any of you who had time to do any investigating found more material than you could possible absorb," said Prof. Tracy.

Most nodded in agreement.

"We aren't going to go into great detail on every point that I mention on this subject, but you'll get a fair picture of how and when the god concept came into play in human history," explained Prof.

Tracy. "I must warn you, as I said last week, I intend to be strictly honest with you in these gatherings, and this subject tonight—the concept of God—is probably the most intense subject we will get into, by far. I want to start with it because it has an impact on everything else we will study in the coming weeks. Whether or not you understand the concept of God, will have a great bearing on how you view everything else we talk about. We will not be discussing belief in God in our study, we will be discussing knowledge and understanding about the concept of God."

"Oh," muttered Jon, "I think you lost me on that one."

"Think of it this way," Prof. Tracy continued, "Think of a ladder, and think of belief being on the top rung of the ladder. Now, you can't start on the top of the ladder, you have to climb up from the bottom. You have to pass through, or gain, knowledge and understanding of a subject before you can form or reach, in the case of the ladder analogy, an intelligent belief. Does that make it any clearer?"

"Yes, I think so," replied Jon.

"Another thought about the ladder analogy is this," added Prof. Tracy, "the knowledge one gathers on the way up this hypothetical ladder must be relevant, current, and able to withstand critical examination. If not, then any belief that is formed will likely be nothing more than superstition at best, and nonsense at worst."

The group sat in silence, all eyes on Prof. Tracy.

"What?" Prof. Tracy smiled, "Did I scare you?"

"Not exactly, but you did seem awfully firm in your last statement," said Ted.

"Well," said Prof. Tracy, "I explained that I will be brutally honest with you and maybe that will come across as awfully firm but rest assured, I don't bite. However, it's possible that some of you might find yourself questioning or perhaps changing some of your beliefs after we update and examine some of your current knowledge and understanding of the Christian religion. Now, let's get down to business. Who wants to be the first to tell us what you found out about when humans started thinking about God?"

Silence . . . absolute silence!

"Miss Burke," Prof. Tracy began, "you mentioned you had read something about totems and spirits. Why don't you tell us about that?"

"Well, . . . ah . . . I read that early humans believed in things that were not really gods. They were, like, spirits or forces of nature. Like, they believed that the wind and thunder and the sun and rain and stuff like that were alive and sort of came and went when they pleased. They had no way of understanding these things and they believed if they pleased these spirits—I guess that's what you could call them— they might be good to them. So that's when they started worshiping and praising and sacrificing to them. And I guess, from there we developed the idea of gods."

"Hmmm, not quite, but that's a good start, thank you Miss Burke, " said Prof. Tracy. "What you just described is called Animism. Animism is associated with our hunter-gatherer ancestors who were around for the better part of the past 200,000 years. We know this from anthropological studies of our ancestors and studies of present day hunter-gatherer people."

"You mean there are hunter-gatherer people living today?" asked Lea.

"Certainly," answered Prof. Tracy "There are tribes of people living in Africa, Western Australia, the Andaman Islands, along the Amazon in Brazil, and a few other places around the globe that still rely on nature's resources and their own survival instincts to sustain themselves. Hunter-gatherers are still with us. Now, who can tell us about totems?"

Jon Parker chimed in, "Well, from what I read about totems, they sounded to me a lot like good luck charms."

"Indeed," said Prof. Tracy.

Jon continued, "A totem might be an animal, or a tree, or a plant, or maybe a rock or carving. Something that the tribe decided was their sacred object. It was supposed to provide them with protection and good fortune. If it was a small portable object, they might take it on hunting trips or into battle with another tribe. I guess they thought it would help them."

Prof. Tracy added, "Scholars and historians debate whether spirits or totems came first. Most likely they co-existed over several thousand years. Of course you are aware that totems still exist in our society today, just as hunter-gatherers do, right?"

"Huh?" Jon replied.

"Sure, they're everywhere, in the form of sports teams and school mascots. . . . The Chicago *Bears*, the Denver *Broncos*, the Tampa Bay *Rays*, they're all totems." explained Prof. Tracy, "Greg, where are you from?"

"Princeton, Indiana."

"And what is your High School mascot?"

"The tiger, the Princeton Tigers!"

"And so your totem is the tiger! Here at Bradley our totem is?"

All together, "Da Braves!"

"Totems—which were human creations some 35,000 to 40,000 years ago—have remained with us, for some odd reason, through all these thousands of years," added Prof. Tracy.

"Okay," he continued, "You've done your homework well. Totems and spirits are considered by most scholars to be where humans began their long journey into the worship of gods and goddesses."

Prof. Tracy went into lecture mode, "The next significant change came thousands of years later and involves ancestral worship, more specifically, worship of deceased ancestors. The spirits of the dead ancestors were worshiped as—what we would call today—gods. In fact, there are stories of the ritual eating of the flesh and drinking of the blood of ancestors to acquire their special skills or knowledge. If my dead granddad had been a good hunter or good warrior, eating a bit of his flesh would transfer those same skills to me, so they believed.[1] These actions or rituals are the precursors of our present-day communion or Eucharist rituals."

---

[1] Allen, *The Evolution*, 124

"Gross!" moaned Sandra..

"Ancestral worship," continued Prof. Tracy, "occurred at two levels of the society. Each family, of course, had its own ancestors whom they worshipped. Additionally, the ancestors of the leader of the group or tribe became the ancestral gods of the social unit—the tribe, the gathering, the region, etc. Most groups probably continued to worship the spirit gods of nature, and maybe even totems, in addition to their ancestral gods.

"Then during the period from about eight thousand years BCE to nearly one thousand BCE, there was yet another change in worship patterns. During this time period, groups invented—and that is truly the appropriate word—gods who were often in charge of other gods: super-gods, most high-gods, gods in the manner of Zeus of the Greeks, Osiris of the Egyptians, or Marduk, the chief Babylonian god. Many religions were formed in this manner, and we call this Polytheism. Polytheism is the worship of multiple gods or goddesses. There are still many polytheistic religions in the world today.

"Other religions—including the early Hebrew religion—recognized the existence of more than one god but worshiped only one. This form of worship is called monolatry, or some scholars might call is henotheism. There is only a slight difference."

"What is that slight difference?" asked Ted.

"Well," answered Prof. Tracy, "a henotheist worships a primary god but might, under certain circumstances, worship one of the other gods as well. Monolatry is the worship of only one god, while not denying that other gods might exist.

"Then came a period when humankind made a great shift in its belief systems. This period began around the beginning of the third millennium BCE. It was a shift from a belief in many gods to a belief in either one god—called monotheism—or to worshiping no god at all.

"Monotheism was first tried in Mesopotamia, later in Egypt and then later yet among the Abrahamic religions. The attempts at monotheism in Mesopotamia and Egypt both failed but the Abrahamic religions—Judaism, Christianity and Islam—continue as monotheistic even today.

"In spite of this shift to monotheism, religions in the form of polytheism, and henotheism still represent much of the modern world. Examples like; Hinduism, Mahayana, Taoism and Shintoism in the East and tribal religions in Africa and South America, are mostly polytheistic and are widely practiced. They remain very popular in their ancestral areas."

Helen raised her hand, "Prof. Tracy, when I went to the Catholic church, we often prayed to saints, like Saint Thomas, Saint Joseph, and lots of others, as well as praying to God. Isn't that just like what you call polytheism?"

"Well Helen," replied Prof. Tracy, "your priest would probably not agree that it is polytheism, but if you look at it realistically, those saints fill the same function as the lesser gods of other polytheistic religions. So, I'll leave it up to you to decide."

Prof. Tracy smiled, then continued, "It is relatively easy for us today to agree that the many gods of the polytheistic era were the product of human imagination. Isis, Marduk, Zeus, Athena, and the gods of the sun, rain, thunder, fertility, and all the rest, were products of the human quest for an explanation of the world around them. Those gods were the byproduct of the ability of mankind to imagine abstract beings and give them, not only a life of their own, but also all manner of shape and size and powers.

"New gods were formed when a group of people sufficiently convinced themselves of the need for a new spirit or god to serve them in a particular manner. After deriving an image of the new god or goddess or spirit and assigning him or her or it the needed powers, the group would develop rituals and ceremonies of worship that were sure to placate the new god and assure his or her or its protection or good will. These types of gods or goddesses and spirits were normally local in nature, belonging to a certain tribe, nation or region.

"And I think we would all agree, they were the product of human imagination, correct?"

Everyone seemed to nod in agreement.

"What we tend to lose sight of," he continued, "is the fact that the God of the monotheistic religions of today, which includes Christianity, Judaism and Islam, is simply a refinement, or more current version, of the man-made gods of that polytheistic and henotheistic age.

He paused to let that last statement sink in.

"I know you probably don't want to hear that, but if you truly want to understand religion and/or Christianity, you must allow yourself to absorb the historical fact that the monotheistic God of Christianity, Judaism, and Islam is just as much a part of the human imagination as were the polytheistic and henotheistic gods of yesteryear.

"So, this brings us to our first great difference between what I have termed Popular vs. Academic Christianity."

Prof. Tracy lit the white board behind him and displayed the following slide,

The Concept of God	
Popular Christianity (understood by people in the pews)	**Academic Christianity** (taught in colleges and seminaries)
God is a supernatural being, "up there" or "out there", separate from the world, that knows all, sees all, and is ever present. He listens to and answers prayers and from time to time intervenes in the world to impose his will and/or perform miracles.	Spirits and gods have existed over the past thirty to forty thousand years of human evolution. They are creations of the ancient mind, a human construct, used to explain the forces of nature, to provide security and to give credence to the moral rules of the group (tribe, village, nation, etc.). They are creations of the mind and exist, in one form or another, in practically every human society on earth.

Table 1

Again he paused . . . there was nothing but silence. He walked slowly to the back of the room, giving the students more than ample time to read and re-read the words on the white board. Then, from the back of the room, he continued in a very quiet and deliberate voice.

"For centuries, the Jewish, Christian, Islamic religions wrapped themselves in the idea that the God of Abraham was different because he had "revealed" himself to mankind. This claim was unique among religions and had the supposed authority of freeing the Abrahamic God from the accusations of being a god of human construct, an imaginary god. The doctrine of divine revelation was used to defend their unique understandings of the Abrahamic God.

"The Jews proclaimed that God revealed himself and his will to Abraham and Moses. Christians proclaimed that God revealed himself and his will through Jesus of Nazareth. Muslims proclaimed that God revealed his will to Muhammad through the angel Gabriel."

Prof. Tracy began to make his way slowly back to the front of the room. "But in recent history, notably the last 200 or 300 years of religious scholarship, the doctrine of divine revelation has been mostly abandoned by religious leaders. Intellectual honesty makes revelation an almost embarrassing scheme. And so, the notion of a supernatural god has become understood in the postmodern academic world to be just as much a human creation as were the gods of the ancient world. All talk of God or of the gods, is human talk. The description of God as a supernatural being, "up there" or "out there", watching over his creation, listening to prayers, and from time to time intervening in the world to impose his will, is a figment of human imagination."

Prof. Tracy notices that most of the students are still focused on the white board. He pauses, then, "Tell me what your thoughts are right now."

Vince Morgan spoke first, "Well, to tell the truth, I wasn't expecting this."

"How do you mean that?" asked Prof. Tracy.

"Well, what that says on the board is that God is just something humans made up, he's not real, just imaginary. That's the way I read it."

"Does anyone read it differently than Mr. Morgan?"

No one spoke.

"I suspect the statement that gods are nothing more than a human construct goes against the grain of what most of you have been taught all your life, am I correct?"

Every head nodded Yes.

"Some of my colleagues have accused me of presenting this information so bluntly and so early in my classes, just for the shock effect. Just to see students' eyes pop out. But the truth is, you will have a much easier time with the rest of the information of this course, if you can come to grips with this concept first.

"I know it's an "in your face" way of getting your attention, but I make no apology. My belief is that there has been too much silence on this issue for much too long. Christian scholars have known that gods and goddesses are figments of mankind's imagination for hundreds of years. But the power of the church and its unwillingness to be honest in its dealings with its constituents has prevented it from revealing such information."

"So, you're telling us there is no God and the church has know this and have lied to us our entire life?" asked Sandra.

"Well, church leaders don't like to hear the 'lie' word, of course," answered Prof. Tracy, "perhaps it's better to say they have just avoided telling you all they know."

"Okay," says Jon, "suppose I 'come to grips'—to use your term—with this idea that our description of God is just a figment of our imagination, then what is the true description of God?"

Prof. Tracy responds, "Let me answer your question with a question; suppose I tell you that the idea of a unicorn as a horse like animal with a solitary horn protruding from its forehead, is a figment of our collective imagination. Would you then ask me for the new definition of the word unicorn?"

"No, probably not" replied Joe, "but this seems a little bit above the level of belief in a unicorn!"

"Agreed," says Prof. Tracy, "and indeed many people have offered new definitions for the word God, but before we move on to that area, let's be sure we understand what I have put before you; that gods and goddesses are human constructs. I'm not asking you to believe it . . . just understand what I am saying. Okay? This is what is understood at the highest levels of Christian scholarship. It's up to you to decide if you believe it or not.

"I want you to think about it individually, also talk about it within your group and we will continue discussion on this subject next week."

"Actually, semester finals begin next week and I don't know about the rest of the group but I need all my time to prepare." said Carol.

"And then winter break starts right after finals." said Helen.

"Wow," said Prof. Tracy, "you're right, where did this semester go? Okay then, I guess I'll see you Wednesday evening *after* we get back from break."

With that the group broke up and went their separate ways.

Lea and Greg walked together across the campus toward Lea's dorm. "So, are you surprised by what Prof. Tracy said tonight?" asked Lea.

"Yes, very much so." answered Greg."This is not at all what I expected. I'm not sure I want to continue."

"But this is only the beginning of the class, there must be a lot more to learn."

"Yeah, but Tracy is sounding to me like an Atheist, not a Christian."

"But he never said he didn't believe in God."

"Well, he said God is imaginary, what's the difference?" replied Greg, raising his voice a bit.

"Are you getting mad at me?" asked Lea.

"No, I'm sorry, it's just that what Tracy said is bothering me. I'm not . . . Let's just not talk about it right now."

Greg knew Lea would want to talk more on the subject but he needed time to process his own thoughts before answering any more questions. They walked in silence until they arrived at Lea's dorm, "I'm going to be at the library studying for finals most of the day tomorrow," he said. "Maybe I'll see you there?"

Lea smiled, "Sure."

They embraced with a brief, friendly hug, then parted.

When Greg reached his room and removed his coat and gloves he took out his phone and texted his friend Jon, "Hey, what'd u think about class tonight?"

Jon: "Interesting stuff. Ted, Helen and I are mtg. at the lib at 9:30 in a.m. to talk 'bout it. Want to join us?"

Greg: "I'll try to be there. Bye."

It snowed again that night.

5

Seeking Validation

The temperature had dropped to 12 degrees by morning. Greg was shaking by the time he reached the library. Helen, Ted and Jon were huddled around large cups of hot chocolate. Greg pulled up a chair and sat down. The conversation was about the weather: the snow, the temperature, and the icy conditions.

Finally Ted changed the subject. "Okay, what is everyone thinking about what Tracy was saying last night?"

"Well," began Helen, "I certainly wouldn't want to repeat it to any of my Catholic friends! They'd tell me I was going to hell for sure."

"Do you believe what he said?" asked Ted.

"I . . . I don't know," answered Helen, "it's really just his opinion, isn't it?"

"Not really," said Jon. "There's lots of scholarship that supports what he said. You can find dozens of books on the history of gods and goddesses right here in the library."

"How do you know that?" asked Helen

"I was poking around last week when we were looking for info about when man first met God. Didn't read any of the books completely, but it looks really interesting and there is lots of it."

"But they're all written by atheists, aren't they?" interjected Greg.

"No way. Some might be, but most are written by biblical scholars or Christian scholars." answered Jon.

Ted mused, "This is not what I expected to hear when I signed up to attend this class but I find it very interesting. I've had doubts about the existence of a biblical sky God most of my life and last night's discussion helped me solidify a lot of my thoughts. This may turn out to be the most informative class I'll take all year!"

"Well, I feel just the opposite." said Greg, "I'm not sure we should continue the class. We're not supposed to be questioning things like the existence of God."

"Are you kidding me?" replied Ted, "Why would we not want to question such things?"

"I've always been taught that doubting or questioning anything in the Bible is a sin." answered Greg.

"Well, I think that's bullshit." said Ted

"Come on guys, let's not get personal. No need to start arguing or insulting each other." remarked Jon, "Let's just discuss the matter like adults."

Just then Lea walked up. She could see that there was tension in the group. "What's goin' on?" she asked, "Something wrong?"

Ted replied, "Your boy friend here thinks we ought to drop our Wednesday class with Prof. Tracy."

"All I said was, questioning and doubting is a sin." said Greg.

"Questioning and doubting is a sin?" asked Lea, "How can questioning be a sin?"

"I'm talking about questioning and doubting the Bible." answered Greg.

"Come on guys," said Helen, "let cool it. We've got tests coming up in the next few days, then we've got semester break. Let's take time to think about this stuff and get back together after the first of the year. I don't think anybody is going to go to hell for thinking about the things Tracy told us!"

"It's not funny, Helen." said Greg.

"I don't mean to be funny, I just think it wouldn't hurt to give this information some time to sink in. Maybe do a little research on our own."

Greg and Lea headed toward the research section of the library. "Boy, you got pretty upset in there." said Lea.

"Maybe I did, but questioning the Bible is something I take very seriously."

"But asking questions is how we learn, you know that."

"Yeah, I guess so," replied Greg, "I'll think about it. Right now though, we better get some studying done or we won't be ready for finals."

—)(—

After semester testing was over, Greg went home for the holidays. It was mid-week and both his parents were working so he took a bus home. A long, boring ride to say the least, but it gave him some time to think. He wanted to leave all the pressures of college behind for a few days. It had been a tough semester.

His parents met him at the bus stop on West Broadway, just a few blocks from their house. Hugs all around and then off to the peacefulness of being home. He knew his buddies from high school would be home for the holidays, too, and hanging out with them was just what he needed to clear his mind.

"You look tired." Greg's father said as they carried Greg's things in from the car.

"Yeah, well, nothing that a few days at home can't cure," replied Greg.

After dinner he flopped down on the couch and scarcely moved until time to go to bed. Maybe he was more tired than he thought.

Next morning he was raring to go. He called his buddy Donny and asked him to come by and pick him up. Donny had his own car. Soon they were wheeling around town seeing who else was home. They picked up George and Charlie and headed to The Palace, a sandwich shop on the town square. In past years, The Palace had been a pool hall and grill, and a hangout for sports buffs. Lots of betting took place— legal and otherwise. The room was always filled with smoke and the smell of hamburgers, and the pool tables were always busy. Recently, however, it had been refurbished and was now a family style eatery. The boys grabbed a coke at the counter and sat down at the table nearest the front window.

"Good to be free of classes for a few days," said George.

"Yeah, except I've got a paper due as soon as we get back, so I'm afraid I'll be spending most of my time at the library," replied Charlie.

Although Princeton was a small town, it had a very beautiful, large, and comprehensive library built with funds provided by philanthropist Andrew Carnegie. Its doors were first opened in the spring of 1905.

"I'm going to just forget school completely for the next two weeks!" said Donny.

"Me too," added Greg, "except for maybe a little extracurricular research."

"What extracurricular research?" asked Charlie.

Greg had slipped up. He hadn't really meant to start a conversation about the special class he was involved in.

"Ah, nothing," he replied, "just some questions I might want to explore for fun."

The boys continued their small talk, catching up on each other's school activities. Donny and Charlie were attending Indiana University in Bloomington, while George was attending the University of Evansville, just twenty-five miles from Princeton. They razed each other about their school basketball teams, girlfriends—or lack thereof—and had a good time relaxing in the familiar atmosphere of their high school days.

—)(—

Friday morning, Greg still couldn't get his mind off the idea posed by Prof. Tracy that God was just a figment of man's imagination. He decided to walk to the library and see what information he could find. It was just eight blocks from his parents' home on North Hart Street to the square and just one more block to the library, a walk he had taken dozens of times during his high school days.

The library was practically empty when he arrived about 10:30. He made his way to the computer containing the library catalog and simply entered the word "God." Scrolling through the results he came across a book titled *The History of God,* by Karen Armstrong. Noting the location, he headed off to see what it had to offer. He pulled it off the shelf and sat down at a nearby table. There would not be time to read the whole volume, but perhaps he could get some information by just skimming through as he did so often while doing research for his classes at Bradley.

On page five he noted the following:

When people began to devise their myths and worship their gods, they were not seeking a literal explanation for natural phenomena. The symbolic stories, cave paintings and carvings were an attempt to express their wonder and to link this pervasive mystery with their own lives. These myths were not intended to be taken literally, but were metaphorical attempts to describe a reality that was too complex and elusive to express in any other way. These dramatic and evocative stories of gods and goddesses helped people to articulate their sense of the powerful but unseen forces that surrounded them.

On page 70:

We have seen that the conception of God has often been an imaginative exercise.

Greg had brought a flash drive with him. He requested use of one of the many computers and began to copy some of the information.

Continuing to thumb through the book he found this on page 397:

Even if we are incapable of the higher states of consciousness achieved by mystics, we can learn that God does not exist in any simplistic sense, for example, or that the very word "God" is only a symbol of a reality that ineffably transcends it.

As he searched further he found more and more references to God as simply an idea, a human construct. His mind was whirling, could this be true? Was his faith being torn apart? Or was Armstrong simply an anti-Christ attempting to disrupt and confuse Christians? He decided to look at other sources. He put the Armstrong book back on the shelf and took one written by Grant Allen, titled *The Evolution of the Idea of God.*

Grant's book provided much of the same position regarding the idea of God, although he went much further back in time and seemed to relate the origin of belief in gods and goddesses to ancestor worship or perhaps, in some cases, totem worship. He found this at the bottom of page 40:

. . . all new gods or saints or divine persons are, each as they crop up first, of demonstrably human origin.

And on page 91:

Normally and originally, I believe, all gods grow spontaneously. They evolve by degrees out of dead and deified ancestors or chieftains. The household gods are the dead of the family; the greater gods are the dead chiefs of the state or town or village. But upon this earlier and spontaneous crop of gods there supervenes later an artificial crop, deliberately manufactured. We shall find that some knowledge of them is needed preliminary to the comprehension of the Christian system.

"This is not good, this is not good at all," Greg thought."How can these people be writing things that are so diametrically opposed to everything I have been taught about God? Can these writers be right, or are they just plain wrong?" Greg was becoming more anxious by the minute. He laid the book aside and closed his eyes. His mind went back to that day he had told Lea he would explain Christianity to her. It was that simple statement that had subsequently spun out of control and led to this moment. He wasn't dealing with this very well, and he needed help.

Just then Charlie's voice brought him back to his senses, "Hey, you doing some of that extracurricular research you talked about?"

Before Greg could respond, Charlie picked up the Grant book from the table. "Whoa, is this what you are doing research on?"

"Well, sorta, you know about that book?"

"Yeah, it was a resource for a class I took last year on religion. Intro to Religion, or something like that," answered Charlie. "You taking a class on religion?"

Greg had wanted to avoid this but now he was drawn into explaining the situation with Lea, Prof. Tracy, the Wednesday night class, and the God concept thing. When he finished Charlie asked, "So, what do you think?"

"I don't know," Greg replied, with a bit of anger in his voice, "I thought I knew, I mean, I've gone to church all my life and I know what I was taught, but now when I start to look at research from scholars from outside the church, I'm confused."

"Well," offered Charlie, "it's pretty clear to me that the weight of evidence falls in favor of the stuff you find here in Grant's book. And by the way, these scholars aren't outside the church, they're heavy-duty Christians."

"I don't know,' said Greg, "I'm not ready to give up yet."

"Suit yourself, but I don't consider it giving up, I just see it as dealing with the reality that history supports the fact that all religions and all gods and goddesses come from the minds of men. I'll see you later, got to get some of my own research done. Good luck!"

Greg sat in silence staring into space for a couple of minutes, then got up, put the book back on the shelf, and left the library. He had at least one more card he could play.

6

Shocking Revelation

Rev. James Hill had been pastor of the First United Methodist Church in Princeton for seven years, a fairly long time as Methodist assignments go. He was well liked by the congregation. He was married, with two teen aged daughters, and the whole family was well entrenched in the life of the church and the community.

It was Tuesday afternoon. Greg's appointment to see Rev. Hill was at 2:30, but he was fifteen minutes early. Reva Lambert, the church secretary welcomed him. She asked how his school year was going and said how nice it was to see the college kids when they came home for the holidays. Greg had known Mrs. Lambert his entire life. She was a kind lady and had been his Sunday School teacher when he was eight years old. They talked for a few minutes until Rev. Hill opened the door to his office and ushered Greg inside.

"So, what brings you here this fine day, young man?"

Suddenly Greg wondered if this was such a good idea. He had thought he could talk to Rev Hill about the God question, but now he wasn't sure how to start. And he wondered what Rev. Hill would think of him. And what if the Reverend told his parents. But he was here now and Rev. Hill had just asked him, Why was he there?

"Well sir, I've got a question, a big question I guess, and I thought maybe you could help me answer it."

"I'll certainly try." Rev. Hill replied.

Greg went through the whole story, just as he had with Charlie, at the library. Rev. Hill sat patiently, with a slight smile on his face. He finished by explaining what he had found in the books at the library that seemed to support Prof. Tracy's contention that God was simply a human construct.

"So, I'm confused Rev. Hill, and I thought you might be able to help me."

Rev. Hill sat silently for a few seconds, gathering his thoughts. He had been caught off guard. It wasn't that he was unfamiliar with the subject; it just hadn't occurred to him that this was what Greg might have on his mind when he had called yesterday and asked to see him. There was no way to ease into the topic when the opening question is: "Is God simply a human construct?"

"Well son," Rev Hill decided to take the fatherly approach, "you're asking a pretty heady question about a very important subject."

Greg sat stiffly against the back of the wooden chair. He was eager to hear what his trusted pastor had to say.

"It seems this Prof. Tracy has introduced your group to this issue without very much background preparation."

"Well," Greg Said, "he told us he liked to cover this subject first, that it would make the other things easier to understand."

"Perhaps, but it's certainly a harsh way to start a class on Christianity,"

However, as he thought about it, it was not much different than what he faced during his first semester of seminary and he had somehow survived the shock. Surely Greg could handle it.

Rev. Hill continued, "To be bluntly honest with you, Greg, Prof. Tracy is correct in what he told you. But let's be as clear as we can about what he is saying. Of course I can't speak for him, but if he were here I have an idea he would say that what he meant was, the concept of God as expressed in the Bible is a human construct."

"But isn't that the same thing?" asked Greg.

"Not exactly. Certainly the idea of a God that lives in the sky, just above the blue, and watches over the earth and all its inhabitants is man-made, but that doesn't necessarily mean that there isn't some other definition for the thing we call God.

Greg thought back to the class where Prof. Tracy had mentioned that some people had come up with new definitions for God.

"But," Greg said, "isn't a new definition just another human construct, same as the one in the Bible?"

"Well, I suppose so." replied Rev. Hill, "But people seem to need a god they can rely on."

"So, what you're saying is—and I don't mean to be disrespectful—the church knows there is no God but they tell people there is one because the people seem to need a God. Is that it?"

This was not going as well as Rev. Hill had hoped.

"It's a bit more complicated than that, Greg," answered Rev. Hill. He was finding himself on the defensive now. "You see, there are a lot of things scholars have learned over the last couple of hundred years that appear to be quite different than what is portrayed in the Bible. And this new information is regularly taught to students in seminaries but it is not regularly taught or preached in the church. I can only guess that your class instructor, Prof. Tracy, will introduce you to much of this new information in the coming weeks."

"Could that be what Prof. Tracy calls 'Academic Christianity'?" asked Greg.

"I expect it is," replied Rev Hill.

"Okay, so why isn't the new information taught in church?"

"That, young man, is where the complication comes in. I will try to explain, but please remember, I'm doing this because you ask. I trust you will understand that it is very sensitive information and treat it as such, agreed?"

Greg wondered if he was getting in over his head, but he nodded in agreement.

"Greg," Rev. Hill began, "if I got up in the pulpit next Sunday and told the people of this congregation some of the things your Prof. Tracy has told you, how long do you think it would be before I would be relieved of my duties as pastor of this church? Christians, or for that matter people of any religion, are very sensitive about their beliefs. And most of what they believe was taught to them when they were young children. So young, in fact, that they didn't question the stories they were being told, they just accepted them as fact. As they grew older, there was no thought of questioning or doubting the stories; in fact, they were admonished not to question or doubt. Those were signs of a weak faith, they were told.

"Today, as a result of several hundred years of scholarship and study, the church has a much more intelligent and honest understanding of much of the Bible and of the creeds and doctrines of the faith, but, for the most part, the people in the pews do not want to hear the new knowledge. They become incredulous when anyone attempts to alter or change what they have believed since childhood.

"I can tell you stories of several of my colleagues who have been admonished or in some cases dismissed from their pastorate for attempting to educate their congregation on these matters.

"The church is well aware that this situation exists, but there seems to be no simple answer to the dilemma. Quite frankly, the answer may lie with people like your friend Prof. Tracy. Most reputable colleges and seminaries today teach the things you are learning in their religion and Bible classes. It will be a very long term answer to the situation, but it may be that our colleges and seminaries are the only places where an honest and truthful understanding of our faith can be expressed without the teacher of the knowledge being run out of town for being honest!

"That, however, solves only half the problem. The other half involves the current members of the church, the ones who haven't been informed of this new knowledge. If they continue to insist that their church preach, teach, sing, and pray the ancient doctrine of the faith, the younger, more educated members of our society will not be interested in joining the church. Surveys and polls are already showing this to be a fact."

"So, what is the answer?" asked Greg.

"Son, I wish I knew." Rev. Hill replied.

Greg thanked Rev. Hill for being so candid about such an obviously sensitive subject and Rev. Hill suggested they might talk again before Greg went back to school.

"And Greg, please, let's keep this conversation just between us for now," he said.

Greg nodded and left the office.

—)(—

There were ample opportunities for Greg to meet with Rev. Hill during the remaining days of his winter break, but he chose not to do so. His mind was still reeling from what he had heard in the first meeting. Now back in Peoria he wondered what he should do with this new information. Rev. Hill had asked him not to speak of it but Greg felt that admonition applied to not speaking of it to his family or other members of the church congregation or perhaps anyone in the Princeton area that might reflect negatively on Rev. Hill. After all, the purpose of the meeting with Rev. Hill had been to seek confirmation or denial of the information Prof. Tracy had told him, and he had explained this to Rev. Hill. Thus Greg concluded that he was free to discuss what he had learned with his friends in the class. This, of course, would sound like a complete reversal of the conservative position he had taken in previous conversations. He decided he would need to find a way to introduce the information without committing to whether or not he believed it. Tricky perhaps, but doable.

He arrived at his room around 4:00 p.m. and texted Ted to see if he wanted to meet at Bacci's pizza. Ted agreed to meet at 5:30.

Bacci's was only a couple of blocks away. The snow was gone except for the piles the plows had made while clearing the streets. Greg breathed in the crisp air. Winter break had gone fast but it was enough: he was ready to get started with classes and complete his sophomore year.

As he reached for the door of the pizza parlor he saw Ted just half a block away. "Hurry up, slow poke—the pizza will be all gone!" Ted gestured!

"When did you get back?" asked Greg.

"I didn't go anyplace. Been here the whole time."

They took a table near the back, ordered a large pizza with everything and continued to engage in small talk for the next few minutes. Greg was sure Ted would be the member of their Wednesday night class who would be the least upset about what he had discovered in his home library and what he had heard from Rev. Hill. So, after their pizza arrived and the serious business at hand turned to eating, he asked the leading question, "So, did you do any research on the stuff Prof. Tracy laid on us at the last meeting?"

"Nah, not much. I skimmed a couple books, one by Bishop Spong and one by Marcus Borg and kinda got the same reading as what Prof. Tracy told us. How about you?"

"Well, I wish I could tell you I found just the opposite of what he told us, but I can't."

Greg went on to tell Ted about the things he had discovered at the library and then, in between bites of pizza, about the lengthy conversation he had had with his pastor.

"So, do you think it's true, that God is just a figment of our imagination?" asked Ted.

"I don't know." replied Greg, "It's hard to believe that billions of people over the centuries could be so delusional, you know."

"Yeah, but if you stop to realize that the whole idea of gods and goddesses came to us from our hunter-gatherer ancestors, it starts to make sense. They had questions about nature and stuff and the only way they could explain it was that there was something bigger and more powerful than they were who was pulling the strings, so to speak. They didn't have the scientific knowledge we have today to explain things."

"Sure," answered Greg, "but science doesn't have all the answers either."

"No, but we're learning more and more every day, and every time we make another breakthrough it eliminates one more thing people used to attribute to God. Take the weather, for instance. In the past, everybody thought God controlled the weather, but today, if you know anything about meteorology, you know that isn't so. And before we knew about bacteria and germs and genetics, we thought diseases were punishment for disobeying God. There's lots of stuff like that. And when we find answers to questions that have plagued us for thousands of years it chips away at the need for an all powerful 'Daddy figure' to be in charge. Chip, chip, chip!"

"But there are lots of things God does," replied Greg.

"Oh, like what?" challenged Ted.

"Well, answering prayer for one. He answers payers, and performs miracles."

"Hmmm, I would argue just the opposite, but let's check with Prof. Tracy on Wednesday and see what he says about that."

The subject moved on to basketball and test grades and other trivia. The two young men finished their lunch, parted, and made their way back to their rooms. Greg spent the rest of the afternoon and evening reviewing material in preparation for starting classes again.

7

The Savior Motif

Lea had not left Peoria during the holidays. She had spent much of her time writing a paper for her sociology class. She spent a couple days touring the Riverside Museum and the Contemporary Art Center, both near the city center. It was relaxing and gave her a respite from her studies.

Now, as the holiday break drew to a close, students were returning, the pace of life was picking up, and her stress level was beginning to rise. Around 6:00 in the evening she texted Greg:

Lea: Are u back?

Greg: Yeah. Where r u?

Lea: Dorm. Want to meet at the Juice Bar in the morning?

Greg: Sure, 8:30?

Lea: c u

Jerry's Juice Bar was located near the Southwest portion of the campus in the Markin Recreation Center. It served bagels, sandwiches, salads, soups and other snacks. A small out of the way place to sit and talk. Greg was first to arrive at a little past 8:30 He ordered a coffee with extra cream and a sausage and egg bagel and since the corner table was open he sat down on the side facing the door.

It was not like Lea to be late, but today seemed to be an exception. Finally at about ten minutes to nine she arrived, bundled like an Eskimo. "Boy, it's cold out there!" she said.

"Yeah," said Greg, "but in a few months you'll be complaining it's too hot, so just enjoy it while you can."

"Well," Lea replied, "I guess that's one way to look at it." She went to the counter and ordered a latte, then came back and sat alongside him.

"So, tell me about your holidays. Lots of fun?"

"Nah, not really, Just chilling out with some of my high school friends most of the time. How about you?"

"I was right here on campus the whole time, so you know how exciting that was. Oh, but I did make one exciting discovery."

"Yeah, what was that?" asked Greg.

"Well, I found a book in the library, *The Evolution of God,* by Robert Wright. It's a fascinating read. I think you'd like it. It pretty much validates all the things Prof. Tracy said."

"Everybody is finding books that say what Prof. Tracy said." Greg's voice reflected his frustration.

"You sound like you think that's a bad thing," said Lea.

"It's a bad thing because it goes against everything I've been taught all my life. It tells me people I trusted have lied to me."

"Did you talk to your parents about it?"

"No."

"Well, maybe they don't know about the origin of God, just like you didn't know before Prof. Tracy's class."

"I hope you're right" said Greg. "At least then I'll know they didn't lie to me. But it still doesn't explain why more people aren't aware of these things."

"If some of the others feel like you do, we ought to have a pretty interesting class Wednesday evening!"

—)(—

By 7:05 p.m. everyone had arrived for Prof. Tracy's class except for Sandra. Lea informed the group that she had just gotten a text form Sandra, that she had been home over the holidays and mentioned the class to her parents and they had forbidden her to continue with the group.

"Really," said Ted, "like knowledge is supposed to be a bad

thing?"

"Some churches are very strict about such things," said Prof. Tracy, "and perhaps her parents are from that environment. It may not seem right for you or me, but it seems right for them."

The group settled into their seats and Prof. Tracy began. "Well, I hope all of you had a grand holiday vacation experience, and are refreshed and ready for your spring semester."

(Groaning!)

"This class isn't part of your accredited studies, but I hope you will find time to give it some serious thought. I believe what you learn here can be very important to your mature understanding of religion and spirituality.

"During our last session I introduced you to the idea that gods and goddesses are human constructs, purely a product of the human imagination. For thousands of years they have been the "go-to" answer for questions for which humans had no other answers.

"I asked you to think about this, discuss it, and do some reading if you had time. So, did anyone have any revelations or epiphanies while you were away?"

After a few seconds, Helen Fredrick began, "I talked about it a little bit with my best friend who is a Baptist and she wasn't surprised. She said she had had some exposure to that kind of thinking in her Ethics class. She had never talked about it outside the classroom because she knew it would be very controversial."

Carol Burke spoke next, "I found a little book titled, curiously enough, *The Dishonest Church*, by The Reverend Doctor Jack Good. He said many church leaders consider this information a threat to the church, so that's why they won't talk about it. He explained that the individual Christian in the congregation is being left behind intellectually and this is starting to hurt the church."[2]

"I've read Dr. Good's book, and it is very revealing. It tells it like it is, for sure. Perhaps a bit to honest for some, but certainly

---

[2] Good, *Dishonest*, 13

honest." said Prof. Tracy. "Did anyone run across any information about redefining what the word God meant?"

"Yeah," answered Vince, "There was a theologian in the 20th century who called God, "the ground of all being," whatever that means."

"That would be Paul Tillich, noted philosopher and theologian of the twentieth century," said Prof. Tracy, "and, yes, it is hard to know exactly what he means by the ground of all being.

"You will find others who speak of God as being in everything. That is called Pantheism. Still others speak of God as being in everything, plus more, called Panentheism. The point being that people are moving away from the simple belief of a God in the sky and are searching for other ways to describe a deity. To me that seems unnecessary but so be it. In my opinion, if you find something other than the sky god that you wish to consider your object of worship or your ultimate concern, call it what it is: love, compassion, justice, or concern for others. Why use the word God and cloud the issue? That's just my personal pet peeve."

"I agree," said Jon Parker, "when someone uses the word God today, you have to ask what they mean by God to understand what they are talking about."

"Okay, I think it's time we move on from this subject," said Prof. Tracy, "My obligation to you all is to explain both the popular and the academic understanding of Christian doctrine, and I have done that with regard to the concept of God. I have no interest in convincing you to believe one way or the other; I'm here to simply inform. Any burning questions before we move ahead?"

Ted raised his hand, "Prof. Tracy, what about prayer, how does that fit into this concept of God?"

Prof. Tracy replied, "That should be fairly obvious, but I'm going to ask you to hold that question for a couple of weeks. Certainly there is an issue here depending on which field of thought you are leaning toward and we'll get to that. Okay? For now, I want to move on to a discussion about Jesus of Nazareth. For Ms Wong's benefit, let me explain. Jesus was a young man living in the first third of the first century of the Common Era. The Christian religion claims he was the Son of God, that he died to save all humans from their sins. Three days after his death he is said to have risen from the grave and ascended into heaven to sit at the right hand of God. His life and beliefs are the reason for the rise of the Christian church."

"But I thought he was a Jew," said Lea.

"Yes, he was, as were all of his early followers.. And for the first fifty-eight years after he died his followers remained a part of the Jewish faith. They were called 'the followers of the Way.' They were a part of the Temple and Synagogue worship. We'll talk more about that later.

"They believed that God had shown himself in the life of Jesus and that Jesus was the new Moses, a prophet in his own right. But somewhere around the year eighty-eight of the Common Era, something happened and they became *persona non grata* to the Jewish faith. They left the Synagogues and began to form their own worship system.

"What I want to draw your attention to right now is what I call The Savior Motif."

Prof. Tracy put the following slide on the whiteboard.

The Savior Motif	
Popular Christianity (understood by people in the pews)	**Academic Christianity** (taught in colleges and seminaries)
The Bible proclaims that Jesus (1) was born of a virgin, (2) was the Son of God, (3) performed many miracles, (4) died a cruel death, (5) died to save us from our sins, (6) was resurrected from the grave, (7) was seen by many after being raised from the grave, (8) was seen raising into heaven.	The Savior motif is familiar to anyone who studies ancient history. Literally dozens of men were marked with these words. It was a way of saying, "This was an important person." Such claims are not historical events.

Table 2

After giving the group a couple minutes to absorb the words on the slide Prof. Tracy began to lecture. "In the study of ancient history we find many so called saviors. Dozens of kings, warriors and religious icons were given the titles Son of God and Savior. Most of them were said to have been born of a virgin. In addition, they were said to have performed miracles, died a cruel death, died to save humankind from sin, arose from the grave, etcetera, etcetera. All of the Roman emperors were said to be saviors, Alexander the Great was called Savior, Hesus of the Celtic Druids who lived around 830 BCE, Mithras of Persia about 600 BCE, Thulis of Egypt 1700 BCE, Indra of Tibet 720 BCE, and the list goes on and on.

"So, let me ask you, do you believe there were literally dozens of virgin births? . . . Of course not. . . . Were there literally dozens of Saviors? . . . Of course not. Scholars, both secular and Christian, explain that these things were written about men of honor, men of high esteem, to say; 'This was a special person, in this person we have seen the divine; remember him.'

"The Savior Motif is so common and so repeatable that even the proclaimed miracles in many cases are the same from one savior to the next—changing water into wine, raising the dead, healing the lepers, walking on water, to name a few. The Savior Motif was commonplace in the ancient world.

"Perhaps two of the most informative books you can read on this subject are, *The World's Sixteen Crucified Saviors*, by Kersey Graves, and *Bible Myths and Their Parallels in Other Religions*, by Thomas William Doane. Both will give you detailed and well documented information of 'saviors' of the same nature as Jesus.

"Some of the most astonishing data you will find, in my opinion, is in the comparison between Jesus of Christianity and Krishna of Hinduism.[3] Kersey Graves lists over two hundred similarities between the two. Keep in mind, Krishna lived three thousand years before Jesus."

---

[3] Graves, *The World's*, 256

Prof. Tracy provides the following handout for each of the class members.

Similarities: Krishna (3228-3102 BCE) & Jesus (4 BCE-30 CE)
• The mother in each case was a holy virgin.
• The earthly father of Krishna as well as Jesus was a carpenter.
• God is claimed to be the real father in both cases.
• A spirit or ghost was the author of the conception in both cases.
• Krishna as well as Jesus was supposedly of royal decent.
• The names of their mothers are somewhat similar, Maia and Mary.
• Both were visited at birth by shepherds and wise men.
• In both cases a decree was issued for the death of the Savior.
• Each had a forerunner—John the Baptist for Jesus, Bali Rama for Krishna.
• Both proclaimed. "I am the Resurrection."
• Each was "the way to the Father."
• Both performed many miracles.
• One of the first miracles of both was curing of a leper.
• Each encounters a gentile woman at a well.
• Krishna, as well as Jesus, was crucified.
• Both were crucified between two thieves.
• Both were resurrected from the dead.
• Each ascends into heaven after his resurrection.
• Many people reportedly witnessed the ascension in each case.
• There is similarity in the doctrines of their respective religions.

Table 3

Prof. Tracy continued, "The stories told about these two 'saviors' are so similar that some scholars believe that the Jesus stories were purposely patterned after Krishna.

"Christianity has continually downplayed or overlooked this part of history and, in fact, there are many stories of Christian censorship and obliteration of scrolls, tablets and codices containing stories of other saviors in order to suppress the memory of such historical events—other than those of Jesus of Nazareth, of course.

"Modern scholarship, or as we are calling it for this class,

Academic Scholarship, explains Jesus in two phases: the historical Jesus, the man who lived prior to the crucifixion story in the Bible, and the post-crucifixion Jesus, the Savior/Messiah that was a creation of his followers, after his death. It is this post-crucifixion Jesus story that contains the Savior Motif. The same is true for all the other so called Saviors. Their stories were written/created years after their death, just as the stories of Jesus were.

"Understandably, this knowledge—that Jesus was not literally born of a virgin, that he was not literally the Son of God, nor did he die to save us from our sins—has dramatic consequences for the Popular Christian faith."

Maria asked, "But why have we been led to believe the stories about Jesus are true?"

"Two words explain it best, Maria—power and control. By the time human intelligence had grown to the point that scholars understood that such stories were myth and folklore, the Church had so much invested in its people believing the stories as literal truth that it could not afford to change direction. So today many Christian churches avoid talking about the literacy of the Savoir Motif. Too much of what the Church professes in its creeds and doctrines depends on the Savior Motif being factual, but common sense will tell you that it is not."

"I've never doubted that the Bible stories were true." said Maria.

"Of course not," continued Prof. Tracy, "I would be surprised if any of you had ever seriously questioned the Bible stories. The Church has done a great job of indoctrinating its followers. It's what they do and they do it very well. Belief in the Bible, as either literal or inspired, is the very foundation of Popular Christianity. It is reinforced in the minds of the practitioners every Sunday morning in the teaching, preaching, singing, and praying during the worship service. And one is made to feel inadequate if one does not believe the right things, meaning the stories of the Bible. It's a great system and it has worked for most of the last two thousand years. Today, however, the Church is in trouble. I started to say it is under siege, but that's not really correct. Siege would imply there are forces trying to destroy the Church, but I don't think that's the case.

"The Church is in trouble because more and more people, like you young people, are learning that there is knowledge that the Church has been hiding for decades. Knowledge that changes how we look at the stories of the Bible. Knowledge that helps us understand the world of belief the people lived in two thousand years ago.

"The age-old message of love and compassion and caring for others still rings true even when we see the stories in a more mature light. The Church, however, continues to dig in its heels and insist that we must believe the Bible stories, *as written*, and that is driving millions of people away. A more educated and informed world wants a more intellectually honest Church, and the Church is not willing to change. At least it has not shown much widespread willingness yet."

"Wow, you've given us quite a bit to think about tonight." said Helen.

"Yes, perhaps I strayed from the initial subject of the evening," said Prof. Tracy, "but we would have eventually gotten to this point anyway. We just got there a little sooner than scheduled. Next week we'll talk about the Bible as the word of God and the miracles of the Bible. That's it for tonight—ya'll have a good week."

From the expression on his face, Lea could tell that Greg was not in a good mood. She walked beside him as they exited Westlake Hall. Once they were alone outside, she challenged him, "So, are you upset again about the things Prof. Tracy had to say?"

"Yes, I'm upset. Yes I'm confused. Yes I'm angry. All those things. Here I am twenty years old and I'm finding out the people I've trusted most in my life have been lying to me. Why shouldn't I be angry?"

"But Greg, Prof. Tracy explained that the leaders of the Church don't know how to tell the world the truth about these things." said Lea.

"I'm not buying that line. Lying is lying and truth is truth, it's not hard to figure that out. I'm sorry Lea, I don't mean to take it out on you. It's just that . . ."

The two walked on in silence.

Finally Greg calmed down and said, "This whole thing started in an attempt to explain Christianity to you and it's me who's learning. I had no idea."

"Well," replied Lea, "according to Prof. Tracy you'd have heard the same things if you had taken a class on religion. So think of it as a positive, you're ahead of the game. Look at how many people will go through life never knowing these things."

"Maybe we'd all be better off not knowing." said Greg, trying to end the conversation.

The wind swirled around the corner of the library building and nearly pushed then off the sidewalk. It was a bitter cold night.

8

More Confirmation

It was not like Greg to be unreasonably stubborn but this was an exceptional situation. He was not ready to give in to the suggestion that the concept of God was merely a man-made concept or that the stories of Jesus were not true.

Rev. H. B Fulling was the pastor of the Faith United Methodist church that Greg had been attending for the two years he had been at Bradley. He felt he knew Rev. Fulling well enough to be able to talk to him about such a sensitive matter.

There was snow on the ground Friday morning. As Greg approached the office entrance of the church, the custodian was just cleaning the sidewalk. "Good morning Mr. Goodwin, up and at it bright and early."

"Oh, hi young man, so are you," replied Mr. Goodwin.

"Rev. Fulling here yet?"

"Yeah, just got here a couple minutes ago."

"Thanks."

Greg continued on. As he entered the reception area he could see Rev. Fulling in the inner office.

Rev Fulling was a man in his late sixties. He had been a Methodist minister for the past forty plus years. Now, he was preparing to retire. He would leave the pulpit in another four months, during the annual Methodist pastor placement process called itinerancy.

He motioned for Greg to come in. "Cup of coffee?"

"No, thank-you." answered Greg.

"Well, you'll have to excuse me if I have one, sort of a ritual you know," he smiled. "What's on your mind this snowy morning?"

Once again Greg related the story starting with Lea's curiosity about Christianity and ending with Prof. Tracy's contention that God was a human construct, only this time he added the fact that he and others in the group had found information in several books that supported Prof. Tracy's contention.

"Can you help me sort through all of this? What can I believe? What should I believe?" asked Greg.

Rev. Fulling sat back in his chair for a moment, then replied, "Your friend Vince Morgan was here yesterday and asked me, basically, the same questions."

"So what did you tell him?"

"Well, first of all I told him, and I'll tell you also, I won't pretend to tell you what to believe, that's for you to decide. But I will tell you what I know and have come to understand. How's that?"

"Fine." said Greg.

"I can understand your confusion, even anger, at hearing these things. Felt the same way myself when I heard them for the first time in seminary. Wanted to quit. Wanted to go out and tell the world that the church was a big fake, but I didn't. I came to realize in time, that the church is needed in our society. Sure, it had some secrets it needed to get out in the open, but I was convinced that would happen fairly soon and all would be well. Well, I was wrong. The Church, and I'm not just talking the Methodist church, didn't come out and talk about these things as I had naively hoped. Too much risk. Not enough consensus about the new information. Fear that the church would lose too many members and that meant losing too much money, and nobody was willing to see that happen even if it meant withholding the information that you have now been exposed to."

"So, the answer was to keep the people dumb, is that what you're saying?" asked Greg.

"Basically, yes, though I probably wouldn't use those words. By the time I came to realize the Church was not going to make any effort to incorporate the new scholarship into its doctrines, I was too committed to get out. I had completed my education, I was married and had a young child, and money was tight. So, I did what many of my colleagues did, I continued to teach and preach what the people expected to hear. The same things they learned from their third grade Sunday school teacher. Pretty soon I just gave up on any hope of a new day for the Church. Many of my preacher friends tried, from time to time, to introduce new doctrinal information to their people, but in most cases they were chastised for doing so by their board or by their Bishop. The word was pretty clear: 'let a sleeping dog lie.' So I did.

"Did you feel bad about that?" asked Greg.

"Yes and no. Yes, because I knew in my heart that there was more relevant knowledge available and by not teaching it I was being intellectually dishonest, and no because I was preaching what they, the people, were comfortable with and what they wanted to hear."

"So, will the newer information never be heard?"

"It's starting to be heard. Groups like yours at Bradley are springing up all over the country. People who are fed up with institutional religion are leaving the church and forming their own study groups. They are reading books written by today's Christian scholars like Marcus Borg, John Spong, Dominic Crossan, Karen Armstrong, Richard Holloway, and others and they are seeing Christianity in a whole new light. If the Church doesn't do something constructive about this situation now, there won't be a Christian Church in the next century. Somehow the Church must come up with a way to combine the wisdom of the Bible with the knowledge of the twenty-first century.

"Let me tell you a story. When my first daughter was in junior high school, her mother and I bought her a set of encyclopedias to help her with her school work. Of course no one buys encyclopedias today because so much reference material is available online for free. But that wasn't the case back then. Well, we soon came to realize that the initial books were not the end of the story. If we wanted to keep up with the world around us we had to purchase a yearly supplement that included new discoveries, new knowledge that had become available in the previous year. And that was something we had to do every year or the reference material quickly became outdated.

"What I'm attempting to explain in a simple way, is that there hasn't been a supplement written to the Bible in two-thousand years! When you hear the knowledge of the twenty-first century laid up against the knowledge of the first century, of course it's going to shock you. It shocked me too. It was like a cannon going off in my head. *Boom*! The Church should have been writing supplements, so to speak, that corrected old outdated knowledge all along. Then we wouldn't have the situation we have today.

"So, I'll say it again, the Church must find a way to combine the wisdom of the Bible—that which has not been superseded by new intelligence—with the new knowledge of the world we live in today. And I'm not sure how, or if, that can be done.

"But I would ask you and your friends to not give up on the Church. The world needs more love and compassion and the Church can be a great teaching resource in our society. Once a critical mass of people come to understand the more mature and intellectually honest nature of the Church's doctrine, perhaps then the attention of the people can be directed toward the teachings of Jesus—where it should have been for the past seventeen hundred years—instead of a belief system that is two thousand years out of sync with reality. We've got to go through this painful process of updating our understanding of the Bible first, but then the door is wide open and you and your generation will hold the key to the future of the Church. I hope and pray you are up to the task.

"Gregory, you realize I wouldn't be saying these things so freely if it weren't for the fact that I'm retiring in another few weeks. You understand that don't you?"

"Yes sir," said Greg, "I appreciate your honesty. I just wish I had known these things long ago."

Rev. Fulling stood, indicating their meeting was over. They

shook hands and exchanged good-byes and Greg exited the office.

Clouds were rolling in from the west. It looked as if more snow was on the way. Greg pulled the collar of his jacket up and walked slowly toward the Bradley campus.

His cell phone rang, it was Lea "Hello."

"Hi, it's me, want to meet up for lunch?"

"Sure, how about an early lunch, like right now?"

"Okay, is Bicca's open?"

"Not 'til 11:30."

"That's only thirty minutes from now, can you hold out that long," she chuckled.

"Sure, see you there."

Greg continued walking slowly, thinking over all he had experienced in the past few months. He felt alone. His mind was telling him he had to make a decision. Either reject the new scholarship concerning Christian history and continue to follow what he had been taught since childhood, or reject what he had been taught and move forward with what Prof. Tracy was assuring him was a more mature and more knowledge driven understanding of the faith. How much longer would he let himself remain in this state of limbo?

His thoughts were interrupted when a large snowflake landed on his right eyelash. No decision would be made today.

When Greg got to Bicca's at 11:25 Lea was sitting on the front steps. "You must have run over here," he said.

"Nope, you were just slow today."

The door to Bicca's swung open and they were invited in, first customers of the day.

After they were seated and had ordered lunch, Greg filled Lea in on his conversation with Rev. Fulling. He finished by saying that perhaps he was in denial, that perhaps he was fighting for something that was, as Rev Fulling said, outdated information.

"You seem more anxious about this every time I see you." said Lea, "I think you would really benefit from reading that book I told you about, the one by Robert Wright, *The Evolution of God*. He not only talks about how humans created the ideas of gods and goddesses but he also talks about how the early followers of Jesus made him into a god also."

"Thanks Lea, I know you mean well. Maybe I'll get around to reading Wright's book someday. Right now I think I'll just try to absorb what I've already heard and see where I go from there."

"But I feel bad that your anxiety is a result of my wanting to know about your religion." said Lea.

"Don't feel bad about it. Maybe this is something I would never have known about if you hadn't been interested in Christianity. Maybe I'm the one who is benefiting the most in this whole deal."

"I hope so," said Lea, "I really hope so."

9

The Word of God

The seven remaining members of the group, along with Prof. Tracy, were assembled promptly at 7:00 p.m.

"Well," said Prof. Tracy, "you must all be anxious to get started. Anyone got anything they want to discuss or ask about the subjects we've talked about in past meetings?"

Helen raised her hand, "Yes, I have a question that's bothering me. How did a concept, like the idea of God that we've been talking about, get to be so widely believed if it's not true? I mean, like, there are more than two billion Christians in the world."

"Good question," answered Prof. Tracy. "Let's see if I can explain. After Jesus died his followers fell back into their practicing and worshiping in the Jewish faith. They became convinced that Jesus was a new expression of that faith, that he was a prophetic voice in the nature of Moses or Elijah. They even promoted that idea within the Temple and synagogue. You'll hear more about that later.

"In the years and decades that followed, this concept of Jesus as the new Moses or Elijah became overlaid with the idea of Jesus as 'the Son of God,' and began to take on a life of its own, *sans Judaism*. So much so, that in the year 88 CE, the followers of The Way and the Jewish religion split. The followers of Jesus found themselves no longer welcome in the synagogue.

"So, the Jesus people went their way, the Jews went their way, and at some point the Jesus followers became known as Christians.

There is much debate as to just when that occurred, but that is not important to our discussion.

"The Christian movement was actually three primary movements and several smaller independent movements by the end of the first century and into the beginning of the second. One was the group of followers originating in Jerusalem, originally headed by James the brother of Jesus, and by the disciple Peter. The second was the group of churches started by Paul, and the third were the Gnostics, who, like the other two groups, had their own ideas about what Christianity was all about.

"The Jerusalem group closely followed the teachings of Jesus and considered themselves the only authentic followers of The Way. They maintained that a person must be a Jew and follow the rules of the Jewish tradition before becoming a follower of Jesus. The Pauline groups were instructed by Paul and did not believe it necessary to strictly follow all of the Jewish personal and social laws. The Gnostics were a group that held beliefs from Judaism, Christianity and several pagan religions from the Middle East and Asia.

"After the Romans destroyed Jerusalem in 70 CE, the group headed by James and Peter began to fade and the Pauline group that existed mostly in the gentile world became the mainline group of the Christian faith. The Gnostics held on for some time, but they too faded under the weight of anti-heresy forces of the next few centuries.

Jon Parker interrupts, "Weren't the Christians being persecuted by the Romans during those times?"

"Yes, they were," answered Prof. Tracy. "Some say it was because they practiced Christianity which the Romans thought of as a superstition, while others say it was because the Christians would not offer sacrifices to the 'approved' Roman gods. We'll never know for sure.

"At any rate, in 313 CE the Roman Emperor Constantine signed an edict called the Edict of Milan that, in effect, made Christianity a legal religion and ended the persecution of the Christians.

Carol Burke raised her hand, "I thought he made Christianity the official religion of the Roman Empire."

"No, that came much later. In fact, it wasn't until the year 381 CE at the Council of Constantinople, that the Emperor Theodosius essentially made Christianity the law of the land," said Prof. Tracy.

"After that, Christianity became the dominant religion of the whole Roman world from Britain in the East and all the nations along the northern and southern shores of the Mediterranean sea. If you lived anywhere in the Roman Empire you were suddenly a Christian. In fact, it would have been detrimental to your health to *not* be a Christian!"

(Chuckles)

"Therefore, Christianity became the religion of much of the known world by edict and not necessarily by choice. Had Emperor Theodosius been a member of one of the other religions of the Roman Empire, we might well all belong to that religion today.

"Now, fast forward to the late 1400's through the early 1600's when explorers began to venture to the New World of North and South America. Where did those explorers come from?"

"Spain," said Greg.

"England and Italy," added Helen.

"Indeed," said Prof. Tracy. "And what religion do you suppose they imposed upon the natives of the lands they conquered? Christianity, of course, at the point of a sword. The stories of some of those conquests depict some of the most ruthless and inhuman violence you can imagine. There is a very dark side of the Christian history of expansion that people don't like to talk about."

Jon asked, "You mean like the stories of Columbus and his treatment of the natives on the Caribbean islands?"

"That is certainly part of it, and there are many more such stories of brutality and savagery by other explorers in other countries.

"That in a nutshell, Helen, is how Christianity grew to cover so much of the world. There are other contributing factors, of course, but we won't go into them now.

"Okay, with what little time we have left this evening, let's take a look at this slide."

The Bible as 'The Word of God'	
Popular Christianity (as understood by people in the pews)	**Academic Christianity** (taught in colleges and seminaries)
The scriptures, i.e. the Bible, both the Old and New Testaments, are the literal or inspired word of God and are the revelation of God to man. They are the infallible, authoritative rule of faith and conduct.	The Bible is not considered a collection of factual statements written, dictated, or otherwise inspired by God, but instead, is a collection of books written by many human authors over a period of more than a thousand years that document the authors' beliefs and feelings about God *at the time of its writing*, within a specific historic/cultural context.

Table 4

"Are any of you familiar with the Pew Research Center located in Washington, DC?" asked Prof. Tracy

(A couple of hands went up.)

"Well, the Pew Research Center is a nonpartisan organization that conducts public opinion polling on a variety of subjects, one of which is religion. They continue to report that as much as 78% of the American population believes that the Bible is the Word of God, and many believe it is the literal Word of God. And, a good percentage also believes it be the 'inerrant,' or error free, word of God.[4]

"One of my favorite Christian scholars is Bishop John Shelby Spong. Bishop Spong is retired now, but he served as the Bishop of the Newark Diocese of the Episcopal Church for twenty-four years, and since retirement has lectured around the world. He is fond of relating the story of a time when he was debating a Baptist minister who made the statement that the Bible was the infallible and inerrant word of God. To which Bishop Spong replied, 'Have you ever read it'?

"The Bible is riddled with contradictions and errors. The very first two chapters of Genesis are a great example. They each give a complete account of the creation story and they are different in every

---

[4] Pew Survey, *Religion and Politics*, Sec. IV

detail.

"I'm not going to waste our time tonight mentioning all the discrepancies in the scriptures, but you can Google 'Contradictions in the Bible' and you'll find hundreds of examples. Hardly what one would expect if the Bible were indeed the literal word of a god!

"If a person has just a small understanding of the history of religion and the ethnic epics of the ancient world, they would be embarrassed at such an idea. The Bible is a compilation of stories that make up the epic story of the Hebrew people and reflect their way of relating to the world around them.

"The writings of the Bible reflect the thinking of many authors, each writing at a different time, to a different group of people, for a different reason. The Old Testament was written over a period of approximately 800 years and echoes the worldview of the Hebrew people during several differing periods of their nation's development. The books of the New Testament, written between 50 CE and 125 CE reflect the early development stages of the Christian church.

"There are many good books in print today that explain the origin and purpose served by the writers of these documents. The idea that they were somehow written or inspired by a god is, of course, ludicrous when one begins to understand the origin of the gods, as we have previously discussed.

"The 'inerrancy' theory is, in fact, a relatively new idea that began about one hundred fifty years ago with the writings of a Princeton University theologian named Charles Hodge. In his book *Systematic Theology*, Hodge asserts that the Bible's moral and religious truths and its statements of fact are all inspired by God. In a sermon given at Princeton in 1866 Hodge stated,

The Scriptures of the Old and New Testaments are the Word of God, written under the inspiration of the Holy Spirit, and are therefore infallible, and of divine authority in all things pertaining to faith and practice, and consequently free from all error whether

of doctrine, fact, or precept.[5]

"Many scholars consider Hodge's statements to be nothing more than a weapon used to defend the church against the scientific knowledge which sprang from the era of the Enlightenment.

"My church," said Helen, "claims in no uncertain terms, that the Bible is the inerrant Word of God."

"I guess I would have to defer to Bishop Spong," replied Prof. Tracy, "when he asked the preacher, 'Have you read it?'"

"If the Church is to be honest with its people it must admit to the human origin of the Bible. The Church must explain that in most cases we don't even know who wrote the various books of the Bible, but it is certain that it was written with the worldview of an ancient people, and does not reflect the knowledge or morals of the twenty-first century."

He paused and looked around the room. They all looked tired. It was time to end the session for tonight.

"Okay, next week we'll touch on the subject of miracles. There shouldn't be any surprises if you think back over some of the other subjects we've already studied. Good night."

---

[5] Battle, *The Christian Observer*

10

The Accident

Greg's cell phone woke him early Saturday morning. A quick look at the screen told him it was his dad.

"Hi Dad, what's up?"

"Morning Greg, Son, I don't want to upset you, but there has been an accident and your sister has been pretty badly hurt."

"Oh my God, what happened?"

"Well, we can go over all that later, right now I think you had better hop on a bus and get down here as soon as possible."

"Is she really hurt bad? Where is she?"

"She's at Gibson General in the ICU. Your mother is there now. You just get here and we'll talk, okay?"

"Okay, Dad, I'm on my way. Bye."

"Bye, Son."

Greg ended the call. For a moment he sat and shook his head, trying to assure himself this was not just a dream. Then he turned again to his phone and called the bus station. The next bus south that would pass through Princeton would not leave until 1:00 p.m. He made a reservation and hung up. Lea's phone was not on, so he left her a short voice message explaining what little he knew and promising he would call her when he got to Princeton and found out more.

—)(—

The bus trip seemed to take forever, finally arriving at 5:30 p.m. His father was waiting when he got off the bus.

"What's the latest?" asked Greg.

"Well, not much change. She is still non-responsive. There is bleeding in the brain. Doctors are doing everything they can."

"Tell me what happened."

Mr. Chambers motioned toward the car and the two started walking, "Becky and four of her friends went to the basketball game in Huntingburg last night. On the way home, just this side of Oakland City, the driver, Lynn, had to swerve to miss a dog, lost control, and ended up hitting a tree head on. Lynn and one other girl died at the scene. Two others had serious injuries but not critical. They are in the hospital. Becky has a massive head injury and a broken arm. They are still checking for other internal problems."

"Will she be alright?" asked Greg.

"It's way too early to tell. Your mother is a basket case, of course."

It was a short drive to the Gibson General Hospital. They parked and hurried inside to the ICU waiting room. Greg's mother was there along with a couple of her friends from the school where she taught.

"Oh Greg, I'm so glad you're here," she said as she hugged him. "Did your father tell you everything?"

"I think so. What is the latest here?"

"Well, nothing really new. She's in a coma, and her vital signs are not improving like Dr. Miller had hoped they would. All we can do at this juncture is pray."

Just then, as if on cue, Rev. Hill entered the waiting room and made his way toward the family. After hugs and handshakes everyone took a seat and Greg's mother brought the Reverend up to date. The Reverend had been with them early that morning but had been gone for several hours.

Greg's phone began to ring. It was Lea. He excused himself and walked out of the room.

"I just couldn't wait any longer, I thought maybe you forgot to call me."

"Actually, I just got here a few minutes ago." He explained the situation and assured her he would call her as soon as there was any change.

When Greg re-entered the waiting room, Rev. Hill was in the middle of a prayer.

" . . . We ask that you watch over her and protect her. Heal her broken body and restore her to her former self . . . Be with this family, comfort them, help them in these hours of trial. These things we ask in Jesus name, . . . Amen"

As Rev. Hill raised his head his eyes met Greg's.

Greg wanted to ask, "Who are you praying to?" but he didn't.

Dr. Miller entered the room and sat next to Mrs. Chambers. "I wish there was something new to tell you but there just isn't. Becky is somewhat stable but her breathing is very shallow. We will continue to monitor her closely through the night. There is nothing we can really do until the swelling on her brain recedes. I suggest you all go home and get some rest. We'll call you the moment there is any change."

Helen Chambers resisted the suggestion stating that she wanted to stay near her daughter. After some persuading she agreed to go.

—)(—

Next morning, when folks began to gather for Sunday School at the 1st UMC, the accident was the topic of conversation in every group. Prayers were said in the women's group, the men's group, and the youth group. At the morning worship service Rev. Hill brought the congregation the latest news from his visit to the hospital and included Becky and the Chambers family in the morning prayer. Needless to say there were many individual prayers offered as well.

At the hospital, all the family could do was wait and wait and wait. Dr. Jenson, the doctor on duty, came by several times to speak with them but he had no new news. Nothing was changing in Becky's condition.

By 7:30 p.m. the exhaustion and anxiety began to take its toll and Leon informed the ICU nurse that they were going home for the night.

"Please call us if there is even the slightest change."

She assured him she would. She allowed them to enter the unit and stand quietly next to Becky's bed for a few moments. Becky was hardly recognizable with all the tubes and monitoring equipment attached to her. Helen was sobbing and holding on to Leon's arm. Greg could feel hot tears running over his cheeks.

The next three days brought more of the same; days sitting in the ICU waiting room, mealtimes with sandwiches and coffee from the hospital cafeteria, sleepless nights at home waiting for the phone to ring, and all of the time, praying for news, any news at all.

11

To whom shall we pray?

The conversation at the Wednesday evening meeting quite naturally centered on the tragic accident.

"It seems so unfair." said Carol. "Young girls just out for the night to watch a ball game and something like this happens."

Maria asked, "Can we join hands and say a prayer for Becky? I think Greg would want us to do that."

They joined hands around the table and Maria led the group in prayer.

"Dear Father in heaven, we come to you this evening with sadness in our hearts. Our thoughts are with the family of Becky Chambers. Please make her well. We pray that you will be with her family, Greg and Mr. and Mrs. Chambers. Hold them in your comforting hands in these terrible moments. These things we pray in Jesus name. Amen."

Ted spoke up, "I don't want to seem disrespectful but just what do people expect to have happen when they pray like this?" He was intentionally asking a leading question.

Prof. Tracy sat silently, letting the group proceed on its own.

"Well," said Maria, "They hope God will hear them and answer their prayer."

"Okay, but in light of what we've learned here in this class," replied Ted, "There isn't a God in the sky listening to all those well-intended prayers, so who are we really praying to?"

"I guess I'm not ready to accept that idea yet," answered Maria.

Prof. Tracy felt he should step in. "And that's okay Maria," he said. "It's a hard thing to accept when you've been taught otherwise all your life. Maybe in time you will change your mind and maybe not, that's your prerogative"

"It's not that I don't understand what you explained about God," said Maria, "it's just that . . . well, if God is just a human construct . . . then, like Ted said, who do we pray to? Or don't we pray at all?"

"Maybe the answer is," said Ted, "we have to learn a new approach to praying."

"I think you may be right, Ted," said Prof. Tracy, "but the old format, the old habit of praying to a father figure up in the sky is awfully hard to break.

"When we pray an intercessory prayer, like the one we just prayed for Becky and the Chambers family, we are asking God to do something. It's like when we were kids and fell and skinned our knee and went running to Mommy or Daddy to have them 'fix it.' Well, the same is true with our prayer: we are asking God to 'fix it.' Am I right?"

"But, Prof. Tracy," said Carol, "there are millions of people who claim to have their prayers answered, every day."

"Yes Carol, I know, but I also know that in every one of those cases the answer to the prayer was ambiguous. In other words, there could have been more than one way the desired result could have occurred, one of which was, God 'fixed it'. The party doing the praying, of course, chooses to believe that God answered their prayer."

"But how do you know that it wasn't God?" said Jon.

"I feel comfortable saying I know because I understand where gods and goddesses come from, and once you accept that reality, then the mystery of why some prayers are answered and some are not, simply melts away.

"Let me tell you a hypothetical story that shows how people find comfort and belief in prayer. Let's imagine a young lady, about twenty-two years old, just finishing her college career and wanting to meet the man of her dreams. She has dated during her college years but has not found 'Mister Right.' Now she prays to God for help, pleading for him to bring the man of her dreams into her life. She wants a man at least six feet tall, blonde hair, blue eyes, sensitive, caring, who wants children, and on and on. A year later she is still praying. Two years go by, then three years, and finally after four years she meets her dream man at church one Sunday morning. He has just moved into town. She persuades a friend to introduce her to him, yada, yada, yada, they start going out, and ten months later they are engaged. She thanks God for answering her prayers. She tells all of her friends how God looked and looked and finally found the perfect mate for her. She is extremely happy. God is good; he answered her prayers.

"It seems like an amazing 'answered prayer' story, right? She had looked and looked on her own and couldn't find the right guy, but in his own time, God found her man and delivered him to her!

"What really happened? Our young lady kept looking until she met someone who fit her requirements—or close enough to them—and one thing led to another and they got married. If he hadn't met her expectations she would have kept looking, but he did and the hunt was over.

"It was a coincidence, nothing more, nothing less. There was no imaginary God involved.

"Coincidences—even remarkable ones—happen all the time. The dictionary defines coincidence like this:

A sequence of events that although accidental seems to have been planned or arranged.

"Answered prayers are always coincidences. They happen to all of us all the time. If you believe in prayer you often handle coincidences like this: if something good happens, you attribute it to God—he answered your prayer or He is looking out for you; if you pray for something and it doesn't happen, or something bad happens, you rationalize that it is part of God's plan, or it is His will.

"If one looks at these events logically and rationally, it becomes obvious that they are simply random events of life.

"Five years and three kids later, when our young lady's 'Mister Right' leaves her for the receptionist in the building where he works, there is no mention of God at all. That did not play well in her plans."

"But haven't there been studies done where people were prayed for and others weren't and those prayed for did better?" asked Carol.

"There have been many such studies," said Prof. Tracy, "but none of them have ever produced any significant statistical advantage that would say prayer made a significant difference. Some have shown a two or three percent advantage for those prayed for over those who weren't prayed for, and the next study might go just the opposite direction. In fact, one of the largest studies of its kind, reported in an article published in the New York Times in March 2006 titled, *Long-Awaited Medical Study Questions the Power of Prayer,* and done with people who had undergone heart bypass surgery, stated that the patients who knew they were being prayed for had a higher rate of complications.[6]

"Let me show you another slide." he said, clicking on the file manager of the computer.

What Does the Bible say about Prayer?
John 15:7 If you abide in me, and my words abide in you, ask whatever you wish, and it will be done for you.
Luke 11:9 And I tell you, ask, and it will be given to you; seek, and you will find; knock, and it will be opened to you.
Matthew 18:19 Again I say to you, if two of you agree on earth about anything they ask, it will be done for them by my Father in heaven.
Matthew 21:22 And whatever you ask in prayer, you will receive, if you have faith.
John 16:23-24 In that day you will ask nothing of me. Truly, truly, I say to you, whatever you ask of the Father in my name, he will give it to you.

Table 5

"Do any of these verses give the impression that only a small

---

[6] https://www.ncbi.nlm.nih.gov/pubmed/16569567

percentage of your prayers will be answered in the manner you wish them to be answered?

"No," said Carol, "but maybe sometimes it's God's will to says no to your prayer."

"If you accept the fact that your prayers can be answered with a 'Yes', 'No' or 'Maybe later', then God answers every prayer. I don't mean to sound sarcastic Carol, but that's exactly how people convince themselves that their prayers are being answered. No matter what happens they consider it to be God's will. You can get that same effect by praying to a door knob.

"How many prayers, do you suppose, have been prayed asking for peace in the world, in say, the last one hundred years? How many have been prayed asking for a cure for cancer?"

"But God gave humans free will. Isn't that where evils like war come from?" asked Helen.

"Helen, without taking us all the way back to the beginning, let me remind you that I started these classes by explaining where gods and goddesses came from, and that should answer any questions about free will.

"However, I would not rule out the positive influence of sitting at the bedside of an ill person and praying with them for their recovery, assuming they are aware that you are praying for them. Positive thoughts do sometimes bring about positive results but that is different than saying that because of the prayer a god reached down and caused something to happen."

"Then how are we to pray?" asked Vince. "Or do we just not pray, period?"

"That's the question most Christians ask when they study the material you all have been exposed to these last few weeks. It's a question I struggle with as well. If you stop and think about it logically, when we pray we are voicing our deepest concerns. The things that are most important to us at that moment. And we are asking God to do something about them. Just because we understand that there is not a god waiting in the wings to do our bidding, doesn't mean that these things aren't still of great concern to us. So, now when I voice my concerns, or pray, I try to do so with language that does not suggest I am asking a god in the sky to do something for me. I am simply expressing those things that are of my ultimate concern. It's hard to break the habit of years and years of asking favors of an imaginary father figure but the change comes with practice.

"I recently heard a statement that was attributed to Pope Francis that might help you. He was alleged to have said, *'You pray for the hungry. Then you feed them. That's how prayer works.'* In other words, if you recognize a problem and you want something done about it, you must take action if you expect the problem to be solved."

"I think I will still have a hard time overcoming my habit of daily prayer," said Carol.

"I understand," replied Prof. Tracy, "I understand."

12

Getting on with life

At 3:41 a.m., Thursday morning, the phone rang. Leon answered. It was the nurse in the ICU, "Dr. Miller asked that you come at once."

As soon as they reached the ICU a nurse ushered them into a small meeting room off to the side of the waiting room. Within two minutes Dr. Miller entered and sat down.

"I'm awfully sorry to have to tell you this, but Becky passed away about an hour ago."

Helen went into hysterics. "No, no, no, oh my little Becky, no please God, not my Becky!" It was all Leon Chambers could do to control her.

Dr. Miller continued, "The monitors told us there was something wrong about mid-night. They called me immediately while Dr. Jenson began to check her condition. It appears her brain began to bleed again, profusely, and there was nothing we could do to save her. I'm so sorry."

Greg sat with his head bowed. He could not believe what was happening. He had not experienced a death in his family before, and this situation was almost more than he could comprehend.

Helen calmed down in another ten minutes and reality began to set in. Decisions had to be made. Family had to be notified. So many dreadful chores faced them.

The hospital's Patient's Advocate came to the room to help the family with the tasks at hand.

—)(—

It would be mid afternoon before Greg thought about informing Lea. He didn't think he could bear to talk about the situation, so instead he sent her a text. Within minutes she responded, expressing her sorrow and saying she would pass the information on to their friends.

Becky's funeral was held the following Monday, at the Colvin Funeral Home. Burial took place in the Maple Hill Cemetery, just a few blocks from the Chamber's home.

—)(—

Early Wednesday morning, following the funeral, Greg boarded a bus back to school. He knew he was not ready to engage in school work yet, but he had already missed a week and a half of classes. Maybe he could adjust better if he immersed himself back into his studies.

The sky was overcast. Sleet intermingled with sprinkles of rain coursed down the bus window. Greg sat staring into the distance. His mind could not seem to accept the events of the past ten days.

Though almost four years separated them in age, Greg and Becky had always been very close; he was her protector. Their mother was fond of telling the story of friends visiting shortly after Becky was born and little Greg telling them, "You can hold my baby sister but you can't keep her!" They shared so much of their young lives together.

He sobbed quietly, tears rolled down his cheeks. His thoughts wandered back to the days he and Becky used to play in the fields on the north edge of town; the winter days they would ride their sleds down the Emerson street hill; the summer vacations they would spend with their parents, traveling to visit relatives in far off places. He was always there to watch over her, like a third parent.

Now she was gone and Greg felt a loss like nothing he had ever experienced before. He had so many unanswered questions: Why had this happened? Why did God let this tragedy take his only sister? Was this part of some divine plan? Where was Becky's guardian angel? So many prayers being said at the hospital and in the church, didn't God hear them? Didn't He care?

Then through the haze of thoughts he remembered Prof. Tracy's words, *"The description of God as a supernatural being, "up there" or "out there", watching over his creation, listening to prayers, and from time to time intervening in the world to impose his will, is a figment of human imagination."*

If Prof. Tracy's words were true, then he had the answer to all his questions: There was no divine reason for the accident, it was just life happening. He didn't know who, or what, to believe. One thing seemed certain, it would take a long time for his grief to be resolved.

—)(—

The bus arrived in Peoria at 1:15 p.m. Greg texted Ted, "I'm back. Meet at Bacci's 4 lunch?" He knew Ted would understand his feelings.

Ted replied, "Already ate but see you there in 15."

When Greg entered, Ted waved to him from a table in the back of the room.

"Glad to see you, sorry about your sister."

"Thanks."

"Imagine it's been pretty hard, huh?"

"Yeah, my Mom is a basket case."

"Well, can't blame her. Must be awful hard to lose a kid."

They placed their order and sat in silence for several minutes.

Finally Ted spoke, "The group will be glad to see you this evening."

"Well, I'm not sure I'm ready to socialize yet."

"Sure you are, it will do you good, Can't just sit in your room and hide."

Greg agreed he would try to make the meeting. After finishing lunch and a bit of friendly conversation that helped Greg adjust a bit, they went their separate ways, Ted to a chemistry class and Greg to his room.

Arriving back at his room, Greg sat down on his bed and called Lea.

"I'm glad you're back, are you okay?" asked Lea.

"I'll be alright once I get back into my studies. Are you going to the group meeting tonight?"

"Yes, want to meet up before hand?"

"Sure, how about the library at 6:30?"said Greg.

"See you then."

—)(—

There were snow flurries in the air as he walked across the campus. It wasn't really cold, cold, just enough to cause him to quicken his pace a bit.

Lea greeted him with a hug that lasted much longer than normal. A hug that said all the things she was feeling but felt unable to say.

Hoping to avoid conversation about the accident, Greg began with, "So, what did the group talk about last week?"

"Well, we started by saying a prayer for Becky, and that took us into a discussion on prayer in general that lasted the whole evening."

"Prayer. Yeah, there was sure a lot of that going on last week—for all the good it did."

"Prof. Tracy said prayer is very important to Christians," said Lea.

"Sure," replied Greg, "until you learn that the God you've been praying to all your life is simply an ancient myth."

"But those people probably haven't been taught the things we have about God. It's only natural that they would pray for Becky."

Greg sighed, "Yeah, I know, it's all so confusing and frustrating right now. What does your religion say about prayer?"

"Well," Lea began, "Buddhists don't pray to a god like Christians. We are more into meditation. Maybe in a way you could call that praying but the purpose is to help us achieve enlightenment."

"What's that?" asked Greg.

"It's supposed to help free us from our desires of the material world."

"Well," said Greg, "right now I'd have to say that makes more sense than praying to an imaginary God in the sky to reach down and heal someone."

Looking at his watch, Greg added, "We better start heading toward Westlake or we'll be late."

—)(—

As the group gathered there were the expected condolences and expressions of sorrow. It helped Greg to know that his friends cared. He couldn't keep the tears from rolling down his cheeks. He felt both sad and grateful for his friends.

Prof. Tracy let the conversation continue for a few minutes before he spoke. "It's good that we have everyone back tonight. We're all sorry for your loss, Greg, and I'm sure I speak for the group when I say, if there is anything we can do, just let us know."

Greg nodded, "Thank you."

Prof. Tracy continued, "Tonight I want us to look at the idea of miracles in the Bible, both the Old and New Testament.

"But first, I'd like some of you to tell me how you would define this word miracle."

Maria was the first to respond, "When I think of a miracle I think of something happening that couldn't have happened without God's help."

"Okay," said Prof. Tracy, "anyone else?"

Helen spoke, "Definitely something that God has done, I agree with Maria."

"But if God is nothing more than a human construct," replied Ted, "what does that do to your idea of a miracle?"

"Well," said Maria, "guess I would have to rethink my definition!"

"How would you define miracle, Ted?" asked Jon.

"I guess I would say that a miracle is something that is so out of the ordinary that no one can explain it, and leave it at that."

"So you don't believe in a god that can perform miracles?" asks Jon.

"I believe that God is imaginary and I don't believe imaginary gods can reach down and alter the course of nature."

Prof. Tracy said, "I think you can tell from this conversation that our belief in miracles is contingent upon our belief or disbelief in a supernatural god. That's why I spoke about a ladder of knowledge at one of our earlier sessions. And you will remember I started our introduction to Academic Christianity with the concept of God. That's the first rung on the ladder. We're on the fourth rung now: prayer and miracles. If you haven't come to grips with the first rung, then of course you're going to have problems accepting the fourth rung—just as trigonometry is a prerequisite for calculus, understanding the concept of God can be thought of as a prerequisite for the other rungs.

"People claim to witness miracles every day, when in fact what they are seeing are simply odd or unexplainable events that occur from time to time in the course of everyday life. Just as it is in the case of prayer, if you look closely you can find other possible answers for such events and having an educated understanding of the concept of God makes it easier to understanding those strange, unexplainable events. You might say they are simply life happening.

"Now, let's take a look at what scholars have to say about miracles, first in the Old Testament, then in the New."

Old Testament Miracles	
Popular Christianity (as understood by people in the pews)	**Academic Christianity** (taught in colleges and seminaries)
There were several miracles performed by "men of God" and by God himself during the time of the Old Testament	Miracles are the product of creative story tellers. They are used to embellish a hero or an historical event with a supernatural flavor. Using miracles allows the story teller to make the characters or the events of the story bigger than life, and stir the emotions of the listener.

Table 6

Prof. Tracy continued, "Scholars have documented 56, so-called miracles in the books of the Old Testament. Some well known, such as Moses and the burning bush and the parting of the Red sea, and some not so well known, like the thunder that destroyed the

Philistines and, the sacrifice that was consumed in 1 Kings 18.

"Such miracles are usually attributed to the actions of an omnipotent god, a god who intervenes to overrule the laws of nature. But since the Enlightenment period that began in the seventeenth century, many scholars and theologians are less likely to proclaim that these are accounts of historical events. There are, of course, many people today who still believe in miracles, but no reputable historian would include in his or her writings, stories of alleged miraculous events. Modern scholars and modern theologians regard such reported miracles as either fabrications or misinterpretations of natural events. Miracles were a vital part of the writing style of the ancient world; however, once again, they cannot stand up against reason and scientific knowledge. Miracles were used in the Old Testament to exaggerate the powers of certain heroes or in some instances to exhibit the power of God. Exaggeration helped in the passing along of oral tradition.

"If one defines a miracle as an act of a god who somehow reaches down and intervenes in the workings of nature in order to favor an individual or group of individuals, then it can be safely said, miracles do not happen, period."

"Boy, I know a lot of people who would disagree with that!" said Vince.

"I'm sure you do," said Prof. Tracy. "Miracles are a very popular subject in the religious world."

"If they don't happen, then, should we just stop using the word miracle altogether?" asked Helen.

"Not necessarily," replied Prof. Tracy. "There is a second definition of the word miracle: 'any wonderful or amazing thing, fact or event.' That definition can certainly be applied to anything called a miracle, without involving or implying the supernatural."

"I doubt that will satisfy devout Christians who believe in the supernatural," said Vince.

"I agree," said Prof. Tracy. "Unless a person has studied the history of religion deeply enough to understand that God is simply a man made answer to the mysteries of life, they are not likely to give up the belief in supernatural intervention.

"If Christianity wants to be honest with its constituency, it must admit that miracles are, and always have been, events that humans attribute to the hand of God, simply because they have no other way to explain or understand some strange or unusual event..

"Let's look now at miracles recorded in the New Testament."

New Testament Miracles	
Popular Christianity (as understood by people in the pews)	**Academic Christianity** (taught in colleges and seminaries)
Jesus performed many miracles during his years of ministry to the people. These are testaments to his divinity.	The miracles of the New Testament are in every respect the same as those of the Old Testament. They are written to extol the virtue of the one about whom they are written. Miracles, if defined as an act or event caused by a supernatural being interceding in the laws of nature, do not exist.

Table 7

Prof. Tracy continued, "Many of the New Testament miracles can be explained as part of the Savior Motif that we studied earlier. They appear again and again in other stories of Saviors written hundreds of years before the life of Jesus. Stories of so called Saviors walking on water, raising the dead, healing the lepers, changing water to wine, can be found in stories throughout ancient history.

"Other New Testament miracles are replications or expansions of Old Testament miracles. They are intended to show that Jesus is the new Moses, the new Elijah. They are an attempt to say that the God of the Old Testament is found in the Jesus of Christianity. Most scholars today doubt that these miracle stories were interpreted as reports of historical events even at the time they were written. It is only with the passage of time and the emphasis placed upon them by our literal reading of the Bible that has distorted their meaning such that some today think of them as literal events. In his book, *Jesus for the Non-Religious*, Bishop John Shelby Spong does a wonderful job of explaining the linkage between the miracles of the Old and New Testaments. I highly recommend it for your reading."

"So," Maria asked, "what about the stories we hear of someone going to the doctor and being told they have cancer and then going back later and being told the cancer is gone. Is that not a miracle?"

"Well, I've certainly heard those stories, too, and I can't explain them. But that doesn't mean a supernatural intervention occurred. There are other possible answers. The first exam could have been a false positive since false positives happen frequently. The patient's immune system may have kicked in and destroyed the cancerous tissue. If the doctor had been treating the problem, the medicines may have suddenly done their job. There can be several answers in such cases. Jumping to the conclusion that a miracle occurred is reserved for those who do not understand that gods and goddesses are human constructs.

"The church of the 21st century needs to educate the people in the pews on the subject of miracles. There is no parent figure in the sky reaching down from time to time to alter the laws of nature to cause a river to stop flowing, or to cause a blind man to see. There has never in the history of the world been a miracle healing of a case of cancer. There has never been a football game won by a miracle field goal. There has never ever been a person saved from death in an automobile accident because God miraculously reached down and protected him or her—never. The church knows this to be true and ought to end its silence on the subject.

"And that's the end of my sermon for tonight. Anyone have any questions or comments?"

After several moments of silence, Ted spoke. "You know, everything you have told us over the past few months, seems to be unfavorable to the Christian faith. When we started the class I expected we would hear things that were different than what we had been taught in Sunday school, but all this sounds more like atheism than it does Christianity."

Prof. Tracy responds, "What I am explaining to you is scholarly information that comes from three hundred years of research and investigative study—critical study if you will—of the Bible and the

Hebrew/Roman world that created it.

"If that sounds like atheism, then you are truly experiencing how great the difference is between what you have been taught all your life by the church, and what the 'professionals' of the Christian faith really understand to be the truth today. I understand that it's a great change; however, the change comes from the fact that we and our forefathers and their forefathers for the past few hundred years have considered ancient folklore and superstition as literal truth. What you're hearing now is a more mature and educated understanding based on knowledge from the world we live in today.

"The purpose of bringing you this information is not to destroy the church; in fact, the purpose is just the opposite. It is to help the church survive and grow in a time when the uneducated understanding no longer works. It's as simple as this: If the church continues to live with two and three thousand year old doctrine it will continue to die, but if it can bring itself and its doctrine into the 21st century, it has a chance to survive and grow again."

The room grew silent.

"Greg, you were not here last week when we discussed prayer, do you have any questions on that subject?" asked Prof. Tracy.

"No, not really" said Greg, "There was a lot of praying at the hospital and at the church, and I know all those people meant well, but I understand now that prayer is really nothing but wishful thinking. Well intended of course, but in the end, if God is only a figment of our imagination, then it is only wishful thinking."

"I would prefer to call it a sincere expression of our ultimate concerns," said Maria.

"It's hard to adjust to the idea that there is not a father figure in the sky that you can call on to help you through tough times, but when you stop to think of it logically and in the light of religious history, it really makes it hard to understand how you could have ever believed such a thing in the first place!" said Carol.

"I hear what you're saying," said Vince, "but in spite of all we've said there are millions of people who claim their prayers are answered every day. Something doesn't compute."

"This can become a circular argument that goes round and round if we let it," interjected Prof. Tracy. "But at some point we have to admit that no one can show evidence or rational reasoning to support the contention that a god has ever answered any prayer of any kind, big or small.

"See you all next week," Prof. Tracy closed his notebook and stood to leave.

13

Original Sin and Atonement

Greg and Lea walked in silence across campus toward the Michel Student Center. They were on their way to the Marty Theater in the basement of the student center. Snow was coming down in large flakes, the largest Lea had ever seen.

"Wish my mom could see this snow, she would freak out!" said Lea, "We don't have winters like this at home."

"Yeah, the snow is nice but the cold, . . . not so much," said Greg.

"Well, if you get too cold I'll keep you warm!" said Lea.

"Deal!" he replied, taking her hand in his.

They walked on in silence; officially or unofficially, it was their first date.

—)(—

Prof. Tracy began this week's meeting in lecture mode, "I know I'm going to repeat myself somewhat this evening, but this point is so critical to the future of Christianity that I feel it needs repeating.

"Intellectual honesty requires the church to tear down the invisible velvet curtain that I talked about a few weeks ago, the one that hangs between the people and the pulpit. It requires the church to face the consequences of decades of preaching and teaching doctrine that is known to be outdated or just plain false.

"There will be pain and anger involved. Many devout Christians will feel betrayed, and some will leave the church in despair. The church will struggle to survive in the wake of criticism and rejection, but in truth it is already struggling because the advance of knowledge is slowly eroding the effectiveness of the invisible curtain.

"Much of this problem could have been avoided had the church been wise enough to advance or revise its own doctrine each time science made new discoveries regarding nature, the cosmos, or the human condition, beginning with the works of Copernicus, Galileo, Newton, and others, continuing down to the present. Instead, paranoia and fear of losing control prevailed, and the authority of church doctrine began to split with reality.

"Today the gap between doctrine and reality can no longer be hidden. Almost weekly there is a new book released authored by a bishop, priest, minister, religious scholar, or college professor revising some element of doctrine or exposing the fallacy of yet another religious belief.

"In April 2010, Rev. Gretta Vosper, chairperson and founder of The Canadian Center for Progressive Christianity and author of the provocative, bestselling book *With or Without God: Why the Way We Live Is More Important Than What We Believe,* made this statement while speaking to a gathering of clergy at the Common Dreams Conference, in Melbourne, Australia."

Prof. Tracy put the following statement on the white board.

We can no longer assume we are the most informed people in the room. Those who had previously believed that everything said from the pulpit was factually true, have, for the last many years, been demanding answers to questions we could easily avoid n the past. Those outside the church, who had all found it too crazy to believe in the first place, have felt hugely vindicated by what they see as us being caught with our pants down or, perhaps more accurately, that, all this time, we have had no clothes on at all and masked that with the bright colors of our vestments and the gilded beauty of our edifices.

Prof. Tracy continued, "If the Christian Church is to be honest with the people in the pews, it must explain in unambiguous terms that the God described as a supernatural being is purely mythological. Anything less than a full disclosure of this fact will only add to the confusion and prolong the dishonest nature of the pulpit/people relationship. If people want to believe in a god in the sky, or fairies, or Santa Claus, or any other make-believe character, let it be known for what it is: human imagination.

"If the Church is to be honest it must admit to the human origin of the Bible. The Church must explain that in most cases we don't even know who wrote the various books of the Bible, but it is certain that it was written with the worldview of an ancient people, and much of it does not reflect the knowledge or morals of the twenty-first century.

"And now that I've gotten that off my chest, let me introduce tonight's subject."

"But Prof. Tracy," said Carol, "aren't some of the things mentioned in the Bible still applicable today?"

"Yes, Carol, many of the wisdom saying and stories are still applicable. And those that are must be brought forward and coupled with the knowledge of our day. Of course there will always be arguments over what is applicable and what is not.

"Now let's take a look at my topic for tonight, the subject known as Original Sin. Are all of you familiar with the concept of Original Sin?"

Lea (of course) shook her head.

"Oh, sorry Lea, I forgot about your Buddhist background for a minute. Let me explain," said Prof. Tracy. "Are you familiar with the story of Adam and Eve?"

"Yes, a little bit," she replied.

"Well, when Adam and Eve ate the forbidden fruit of a particular tree in the garden of Eden, Christian doctrine says that this was the first or Original Sin of humankind. This first sin, an action of the first human beings, is traditionally understood to be the cause of the fallen state from which human beings can be saved only by God's grace.

"You may be surprised to learn that the doctrine of original sin is not found in the Bible. It was first developed in the second century by a man named Saint Irenaeus, the Bishop of Lyon in southern France. The concept of original sin was further developed centuries later by Saint Augustine of Hippo in Algeria, North Africa. Augustine is probably the most important figure in the development of the concept of Original Sin. He taught that Original Sin was physically transmitted from parent to child through reproduction.

"In Augustine's view, all of humanity was present in Adam when he sinned, and therefore all humans are sinners. Original sin, according to Augustine, consists of the guilt of Adam which all human beings inherit. So, as sinners, we human beings are utterly depraved in nature, and can only be redeemed by the grace of God

"St. Augustine believed that the only possible destinations for the human soul are heaven and hell. He believed that infants, who die before being baptized, go to hell as a consequence of Original Sin.

"Well, Prof. Tracy, where did Augustine get this information if it isn't in the Bible?" asked Vince.

"There is no source mentioned in any writing that I am aware of, other than the mind of St. Augustine himself," answered Prof. Tracy.

"St. Augustine's idea of Original Sin became popular within the Roman Catholic Church and much later among Protestant reformers like Martin Luther and John Calvin. But like other traditional church doctrines, Original Sin has been denied or reinterpreted by various modern Christian denominations and theologians.

"Think about it . . . what we have here is an imaginary god, an imaginary creation story, a 'perfect' man and woman, and a talking snake, all coming together in an imaginary garden. Then thousands of years later, some zealous religious leader concluded that the actions of this rebellious, imaginary man and woman have somehow been passed down from generation to generation to every man, woman, and child that has ever been or ever will be born.

"Original Sin is nothing more than a human idea, a doctrine invented by those who were promoting the Christian religion. Its original intent, in my opinion, might well have been to induce fear in the masses and cause them to flock to the church to seek redemption. This brings us to our next topic, Atonement.

"But first, are there any questions or discussion on Original Sin?"

Ted responded, "Well, not exactly Original Sin, but I thought I heard you say imaginary creation story. I take it then, you are saying creationism is imaginary also?"

"Yes," answered Prof. Tracy. "both creation stories in the Bible are folklore, not history."

"*Both* stories?" asked Ted.

"Yes," said Prof. Tracy. "If you'll remember I mentioned the fact that there were two creation stories in one of our earlier meetings. Beginning with Genesis 1:1, and running to Chapter 2:4, is one story, and then the second story takes up the rest of Chapter 2 from verse 5 to the end of the Chapter."

"But why two?" asked Lea.

"The first story was written by someone, probably a priest, living in the Northern Kingdom of Israel and it reflects the folklore stories as they were told in that area. The second story, essentially Chapter 2, was written by someone in the Southern Kingdom of Judea and likewise reflects the folklore of that area. After the Northern Kingdom was overrun by the Assyrians, sometime around 722 BCE, a remnant of the people from the North migrated to the South and, of course, brought their folklore with them. Without going into too much detail, sometime later the two versions of Genesis were combined. Most of the stories that appear in Chapters 3 through 50 are melded together in such a way that most people don't realize they are actually reading two stories. Chapters 1 and 2, however, were left intact and appear one following the other.

"Another bit of interesting information about those two stories is that Chapter 2, the one written in the South, was written about 950 BCE, whereas the Chapter 1 was written somewhere around 800 to 825 BCE, some 100 plus years later. I don't know why they appear in reverse order."

"Maybe that's where we get the expression, 'The first will be last and the last will be first'!" quipped Jon.

Everyone chuckled.

"No, not really, but that does appear in the Bible!" said Prof. Tracy. "Now, if there are no more questions, let's move on to the idea of atonement."

Prof. Tracy put up the following slide:

Atonement	
Popular Christianity (as understood by people in the pews)	**Academic Christianity** (taught in colleges and seminaries)
Jesus was sent by God from heaven to earth, to suffer and die as a sacrifice for the sins of all mankind. This was the central purpose of the life and death of Jesus.	The first mention of the idea of Jesus dying for the sins of mankind appears in the writings of Paul (1Thes 5:10,Gal 1:4, 1 Cor 8:11, 2 Cor 5:14-15, Rom 5:6-8). The concept of atonement was later expounded upon by St. Augustine of Hippo, a fifth-century theologian. It is a manmade concept.

Table 8

He began his lecture. "In the Old Testament, the Day of Atonement was an annual day of repentance for the people of Israel, a day to ask God for the forgiveness of their sins. The ritual of Atonement is prescribed in the Old Testament book of Leviticus Chapter 16, also Leviticus 23, Leviticus 25, Exodus 30, and Numbers 29. It is described as a solemn fast, during which no food or drink could be consumed, and all work was forbidden.

"During the ritual, the high priest was to offer an animal sacrifice upon the altar, as an atonement a forgiveness of sins for himself and for the people. The Bible calls this, *Yom Hakippurim* Hebrew for Day of Atonement which the Jewish religion celebrates today as *Yon Kippur.*

"Now, hold that thought while we look at another Jewish holiday, called Pasach in Hebrew or Passover in English, which celebrates and remembers the freeing of the Hebrews from slavery in ancient Egypt. The origin of this story appears in Exodus Chapter 12. The Hebrews had been held as slaves in Egypt for several hundred years, and God allegedly chose Moses to lead them out of bondage. Moses repeatedly asked the Pharaoh of Egypt to let the people of Israel leave his land, but God hardened Pharaoh's heart and he repeatedly refused. As a result, God caused a series of plagues to come upon Egypt. Lea, I know some of this is probably beyond your knowledge of Christianity, but please bear with me. I think you'll understand the point I am making soon enough."

Lea smiled in agreement.

"In the tenth and final plague, God caused an angel of death to pass over the entire land of Egypt and kill the firstborn offspring of every household, both humans and animals. To provide protection from this angel of death for the children of Israel, God instructed the Hebrew people to sprinkle the blood of a sacrificed lamb on the two side doorposts of their houses and on the upper doorpost, called the lintel. The angel, upon seeing the blood, would 'pass over' that house and not destroy its firstborn. Hence, the sacrificial lamb was called the Passover lamb. In carrying out this commandment from God to use the slain lamb, the Hebrew people protected themselves from the angel of death.

"This alleged slaughter of the firstborn of the Egyptians seemed to convince the Pharaoh that God was serious and he subsequently let the Hebrews go!

"Later, as Moses was leading the Hebrews through the wilderness of the Sinai, God commanded that they should, according to Numbers 9:3, celebrate and remember the event of the 'passover' annually. Thus the celebration called Pasach or Passover came into being and is still celebrated today among the Jewish communities of the world.

"Now, fast forward from roughly 1250 BCE in the Old

Testament to the year 56 CE, in the New Testament, to the day Saint Paul's letter to the church at Corinth was received by that little group of followers. We call the letter 1st Corinthians. We don't actually know how little or big the group at Corinth was. It could have been six people, or it could have been sixty. We just don't know.

"On that day, the people gathered either in the synagogue, or perhaps someone's home, or maybe in some public place to have one of their number read this letter, just received, from this self-proclaimed itinerant preacher/apostle named Paul.

"In 56 CE the church at Corinth was having problems. Apparently discipline problems among its members were rampant. Paul was writing in an attempt to get them to straighten up, and get their act together, so to speak.

"I'll not read the entire letter, just one sentence from Chapter 5 where he writes,

For our Passover feast is ready, now that Christ, our Passover lamb, has been sacrificed.

"Paul was likening Jesus to the Passover lamb that the Hebrews sacrificed each year in remembrance of their protection from the angel of death. But as we discover by reading further, Paul was also calling Jesus the sacrificial lamb that released us, all humankind, from the bondage of both sin and death. He seems to be combining the meaning of the two separate events in Hebrew history, into one—Atonement, the forgiveness of sin, and Passover, release from the power of death.

"I'm not quite old enough, but, had I been there that day in 56 CE, I think I would have spoken up at that point and said to the reader, 'Wait, wait . . . read that part again, please.'

For our Passover feast is ready, now that Christ, our Passover lamb, has been sacrificed.

"I may have stood and listened in silence to the rest of the letter, but then I think I would have hurried to my home and searched for a piece of parchment, and I would have penned a letter to be carried back to Saint Paul who had written from Ephesus in Asia Minor. I would have written something like this:

'Dear Sir,
We just finished the reading of your letter. Thank you for your concern for the people of Corinth. It is very kind of you. However, I have one question. By what authority have you called this man Jesus, our Passover lamb? Where did you come by the idea that he was sacrificed for us?'

"To me, this is a very important question, because on Paul's simple statement hinges the entire church doctrine of Atonement and Salvation. Paul made a giant leap to proclaim Jesus to be the Passover lamb, with the unexplained twist that, whereas the Passover lamb had triggered the Hebrew's protection from the angel of death and freedom from the Egyptians, Jesus as Passover lamb had freed all humans, for all time, from both sin and death. Paul said it, the people accepted it— apparently without question—and for the ensuing two thousand years, it has dominated the doctrine of the Christian church. It has been called the centerpiece of the Christian faith.

"But I would ask him, by what authority, what special knowledge, what evidence did he make such a self serving, egocentric proclamation? The answers, of course, are none, none, and none! No authority, no special knowledge, and no evidence."

"So, where *did* he get this information?" asked Helen.

"Good question Helen . . . where could Paul have gotten such a story? Did he make it up? Did he have a dream? Did this thought come to him through meditation or prayer? Did he base it on his interpretation of some portion of ancient scripture? Was it a part of the oral tradition of the day? We are not given any indication of any of these possibilities. Yet the church has followed this vague line of delusional thinking ever since.

"I wish I could have had the opportunity to query Paul about that statement and the similar statements he made to the Galatians, the Thessalonians, the Romans, and others.

"Perhaps Paul, knowing that many nations and many other religions of that era had deemed certain of their heroes Saviors, thought it would be quite all right for him to promote Jesus to the same status. You remember the Savior Motif we talked about in an earlier meeting; It was not an uncommon practice. If he could convince people to believe such a thing it would certainly strengthen his cause as well.

"Paul wrote nothing of the teachings of Jesus, only that he died for the salvation of all humankind. Something that was totally foreign to anything Jesus had ever said or taught.

"So, by what authority did he declare these things to be true? By what special knowledge? By what evidence? Unfortunately the answers still seem to be . . . none . . . none . . . and none!

"Some scholars accuse Paul of kidnapping the church with his idea of atonement and salvation. The idea is diametrically opposed to the teachings of Jesus. Jesus taught us to care for others. He taught us to help the poor, to reach out to the downtrodden and those at the fringe of society, to seek justice for all people. Yet in all of the thirteen books of the New Testament attributed to Paul, there is not a word about the teachings of Jesus.

"The leaders of the new movement in Jerusalem, James and Peter, espoused a doctrine that seemed to follow the teachings of Jesus, but once the Jesus movement split from the Jewish religion for good in 88 CE, the Pauline version became dominant and has remained so ever since.

"In my opinion, the church needs to come to grips with the myth of atonement. It needs to begin to speak honestly with the people in the pews of our churches about this ancient belief—where it came from and why it was so appealing to the Gentile world. The church needs to assure all Christians that each human is responsible for his or her own behavior. No one has died to redeem another for their actions. Atonement, like so many of the church's doctrines, is a purely human construct."

"Seems logical to me," said Jon. "If God is a human construct and the creation story is folklore and Original Sin is manmade, the idea of a man dying for the sins of all the people of the world for all time seems pretty made up."

"These were people who believed that they could put their sins on the back of a lamb and God would forgive them," said Vince.

"Poof! There goes another ancient doctrine out the window!" said Ted.

"Remember," said Prof. Tracy, "the people at that time were searching for answers to life's mysteries, just the same as we are today. Only they didn't have all the tools of knowledge that we have today. Think about that before you speak too harshly of them."

"And who knows," remarked Carol, "a thousand years from now, the things we consider true today may seen out of touch with reality also."

"That's very true," said Prof. Tracy.

14

The Trinity

P rof. Tracy turned to another subject.
"Perhaps the most interesting, most absorbing, and at the same time the most confusing item of Christian doctrine, is called the Holy Trinity. Many church leaders feel the Trinity is one of the most important doctrines of the Christian religion. Nearly all Christian churches agree that the Trinity is a fundamental doctrine of Christianity.

"The confusion for me, and I suspect for you as well, comes in our attempt to conceptualize the idea of this very important doctrine, which, when simply stated says: God is triune, that is, the Father is totally God, the Son is totally God, the Holy Spirit is totally God, and yet, there are not three Gods but only one. Each is said to be without beginning, having existed for eternity. Each is said to be almighty, with each neither greater nor lesser than the other, and yet they are only one.

"The people in the pews of many churches sing of this Holy Trinity in the hymn called the Doxology: *Praise God from whom all blessings flow, / Praise him all creatures here below, / Praise him above ye heavenly hosts, / Praise Father, Son and Holy Ghost.*

"As a youngster, I often thought that referring to the Holy Spirit as *the Holy Ghost* was border-line blasphemy but I guess not, it's in our hymn books and other religious documents. Yet I always felt uncomfortable about the phrase *Holy Ghost*. Not nearly as uncomfortable, however, as when some of my friends in our youth group would refer to the Trinity as, 'Daddy-o, JC, and the spook!' But that's another story."

They all laughed together.

Prof. Tracy put the following chart on the white board:

The Trinity	
Popular Christianity (as understood by people in the pews)	**Academic Christianity** (taught in colleges and seminaries)
Christian doctrine holds that God is one, but that three distinct "persons" constitute the one God: the Father, the Son, and the Holy Spirit. This threefold God of Christian belief is referred to as the Trinity.	The word Trinity is found in neither the Old nor the New Testament. The idea of the Trinity did not appear until the fourth century CE. It is a human concept and has no basis in reality.

Table 9

"The Encyclopedia Americana notes that the doctrine of the Trinity is considered to be '*beyond the grasp of human reason*'. Joseph Bracken mirrors that statement in his book, *What Are They Saying About the Trinity?* when he writes,

> *Christian professionals who with considerable effort learned about the Trinity during their seminary years hesitate to present it to their people from the pulpit, even on Trinity Sunday. Why should they bore people with something that in the end they wouldn't properly understand anyway.* [7]

"Perhaps then, with all of this, you and I don't need to feel uneasy if we are somewhat confused by this rather unwieldy doctrine. But inquiring minds want to know, and I, for good or ill, have one of those inquiring minds. So one day I began to have questions about the Trinity. One of my first questions was, 'How did such a confusing doctrine originate?' Little did I know where that question would lead me.

---

[7] Bracken, What Are They Saying, 3

"My first inclination was to turn to the Bible. Surely the Bible would clearly reveal information about a matter as fundamental as the Trinity is claimed to be. But I was amazed to discover that the word Trinity is not found in the Bible.

"Okay, but while the word Trinity is not found in the Bible, perhaps at least the *idea* of the Trinity is there. Well, the Encyclopedia of Religion states: '*Theologians today are in agreement that the Hebrew Bible does not contain a doctrine of the Trinity.*' [8] And the New Catholic Encyclopedia also states: '*The doctrine of the Holy Trinity is not taught in the Old Testament.*' [9]

"Edmund Fortman, in his book *The Triune God* writes this:

'*The Old Testament writings about God neither express nor imply any idea of, or belief in, a plurality or trinity of persons within the one Godhead.*' [10]

"So then, what about the Christian Scriptures, or New Testament as they are known. Do they speak of a Trinity?
"The Encyclopedia Britannica states: '*Neither the word Trinity nor the explicit doctrine appear in the New Testament.*' [11] In his book, *A Short History of Christian Doctrine* author Bernhard Lohse says: '*As far as the New Testament is concerned, one does not find in it, an actual doctrine of the Trinity.*' [12]

"So, I discovered, neither the thirty-nine books of the Hebrew Scriptures nor the twenty-seven books of the Christian Scriptures provide any teaching of the Trinity. To say the least, I was surprised. But if the Trinity is not a Biblical teaching, how did it become a

---

[8] LaCugna, "*Trinity*," Vol. 14, 9360

[9] Driana, "*Holy Trinity,*" Vol. 14, 201

[10] Fortman, *The Triune God,* 9

[11] Encyclopedia Britannica, *Trinity,* Vol. 11, 928

[12] Lohse, *A Short History,* 38

Christian doctrine?

"Well, I discovered that some people believe it happened at the Council of Nicaea, in Greece, in the year 325 CE. But that is not totally correct. The Council of Nicaea did state that Jesus was made *'of the same substance'* as God, but it did not establish the Trinity.

"The Roman Emperor Constantine had called the Council of Nicaea. Constantine was aware there was a debate in the church over the issue of the divinity of Jesus, and he surmised that such a religious division was a threat to his empire. So he called the bishops together to settle the issue once and for all. But after two months of debate, the 318 bishops in attendance took a vote and declared that Jesus was *'of one substance with the Father.'* So remember, none of the debate at Nicaea was over the issue of a Trinity, it was about the divinity of Jesus.

"After Nicaea, the debate about Jesus continued for decades. Those who believed that Jesus was *not* of the same substance as God actually came back into favor for a period of time. But then in 381 CE, Emperor Theodosius convened yet another Church Council, this one in Constantinople, to clarify once again that Jesus *was* of the same substance as God.

"It was at this Council in 381 CE, that the bishops decided to place the Holy Spirit on the same level as God. And so for the first time, Christianity's Trinity began to come into focus. It did not appear as part of a creed, however, until somewhere in the late fifth or early sixth century when the Athanasian creed is first reported to have been used."

"So, who were these men who decided all this stuff about the Trinity?" asked Maria.

"Well, Maria, to answer that question,—Who were these men?—let's try to travel back to the fourth century for a minute or two. The worldview of that era was quite different than the worldview of today. People of that era believed the earth was flat, that it rested on a bed of water, and the blue sky above was a canopy beyond which was heaven and the almighty God. And this blue canopy was just a few hundred feet above us.

"To be literate in the fourth century CE meant you could spell your name! That might be a slight exaggeration, but certainly no more than four or five percent of the population were literate.

"Few churches possessed a Bible. Most religious understanding was passed from person to person through oral tradition. This accounts for the many diverse beliefs within Christianity in that era.

"The bishops of the church were, of course, men who held this same worldview. Perhaps educated by the standards of that time and place, but certainly not intellectually astute by today's standards.

"The bishops of the church certainly had the authority to decide for the church what the church would believe as doctrine—after all they were the bishops—but as far as their ability to decide that such a thing as the Trinity was true, factual, or physically correct, they had absolutely no such knowledge whatsoever. They performed no investigation, no experiments, no DNA tests. They simply debated the issue, took a vote, and proclaimed it to be true. There was absolutely nothing to substantiate such a claim.

"These unnamed, unknown men who were, by today's standards semi-literate at best, simply decreed that it was so, and for the ensuing 1600 years we Christians have believed as literal truth, that the Father, the Son and the Holy Spirit are all of the same substance, not three but one, not one but three, excreta, excreta, *ad nauseam.*

"There are many stories like the one about the Trinity. The Church history is replete with legends and symbols, that you and I, the people in the pews, have been taught to believe as literal truth but in fact have no validity beyond their human source.

"The real message of the Trinity lies not in the Trinity itself, but behind the Trinity, in the reason why those ancient bishops felt compelled to relate such a story."

"Poof, poof, there goes another doctrine out the window!" said Ted.

"Ted, aren't you being a bit callous about this?" said Helen, "I mean, this is quite shocking information to some of us."

"Gee, I'm sorry, didn't mean to offend."

"It's shocking to hear information like this that tends to destroy things you've believed all your life. It leaves you feeling empty."

"What ticks me off," says Jon, "is that the Church has known these things for so long and still isn't being honest about them."

Prof. Tracy interrupts, "Remember what I told you about the clergy. Most of those who have been taught the things I have explained to you would love to be honest with their congregations, but the fear of losing their job holds them back.

"Let me read you something if I can find it here." He fumbles through his briefcase. Pulling out a small folder he opens it and begins to read.

"In 2010 the journal *Evolutionary Psychology* published an article titled, 'Preachers who are not believers'" [13]

He looks around the room. All eyes are on him.

"The article was the report of a study made possible by a grant from a small foundation administered through Tufts University. The study was conducted by Ms Linda LaScola, a clinical social worker with years of professional experience as a qualitative researcher and psychotherapist, and philosopher Daniel Dennett, the author of *Breaking the Spell*.

"The abstract of the study states the researchers' belief:

There are systemic features of contemporary Christianity that create an almost invisible class of non-believing clergy, ensnared in their ministries by a web of obligations, constraints, comforts, and community.

The study then sets out to answer the question: *'Are there clergy who don't believe in God?'*

"For the study the researchers identified five brave pastors, all still actively engaged with parishes, who were willing to tell their stories. All five were Protestants, with master's level seminary education. Three

---

[13] Dennett and LaScola, *Preachers*, 120-150

represented liberal denominations and two came from more conservative, evangelical traditions.

"Here are excerpts from two of the interviews.

"Darryl, a thirty-six-year-old Presbyterian minister with a church outside of Baltimore wrote this:

> *I am interested in this study because I have regular contact in my circle of colleagues—both ecumenical and Presbyterian—who are also more progressive-minded than the "party line" of the denomination. We are not "un-believers" in our own minds—but would not withstand a strict "litmus test" should we be subjected to one. I want to see this new movement within the church given validity in some way. I reject the virgin birth. I reject substitutionary atonement. I reject the divinity of Jesus. I reject heaven and hell in the traditional sense, and I am not alone.*

Prof. Tracy pauses and looks around the room again. The group is still sitting in absolute silence, fixated on every word. He continues reading.

"Adam, a forty-three-year-old worship minister and church administrator in a large Church of Christ congregation in South Carolina, although raised Presbyterian, became involved with conservative Christianity. Even in seminary, when confronted with questions and contradictions in the study of academic Christianity, he stayed focused on his desire to help people live a Christian life that would ultimately lead them to eternal life.

"Today, however, he struggles through his job, hiding his true beliefs. Here's what he says,

> *Here's how I'm handling my job on Sunday mornings: I see it as play acting. I kind of see myself as taking on a role of a believer in a worship service, and performing. Because I know what to say. I know how to pray publicly. I can lead singing. I love singing. I don't believe what I'm saying anymore in some of these songs. But*

I see it as taking on the role and performing. Maybe that's what it takes for me to get myself through this, but that's what I'm doing.

I'm where I am because I need the job. Still, if I had an alternative, a comfortable paying job, something I was interested in doing, and a move that wouldn't destroy my family, that's where I'd go. Because I do feel kind of hypocritical. It used to be the word "hypocritical" was like a sin. I don't hold that view anymore: there is goodness, and there is sinfulness; it's one or the other. It's black or white. That there's ultimate absolute truths that are mandated in scripture or given by a supernatural being. I don't see those anymore, so I use the word "hypocritical" differently, as in, I'm just not being forthright. But, at the same time, I'm in the situation I'm in, and rationally thinking about it is what I've got to do right now.

I've got to the point where I can't find meaning in something that I don't think is real anymore. I guess mostly inside I do toy with the fact that, 'OK, what's driving me to get up every morning?' I used to be very devotional-minded. Get up, and maybe read a passage of scripture; say a prayer; ask God to guide me through the day, totally believing that he would. Now it's like, 'You don't have that anymore.' So there's a lack of guidance. But at the same time I find it more free, where I create my own day.

"When researchers asked one of the other pastors they talked with if he thought clergy with his views were rare in the church, he responded, *'Oh no, you can't go through seminary and come out believing in God.'* Surely an overstatement, but a telling one. As Wes put it:

. . . there are a lot of clergy out there who—if you were to ask them—if you were to list the five things that you think may be the most central beliefs of Christianity, they would reject every one of them.

"I think that's what saddens me the most." said Maria, "The idea that there are pastors out there, maybe even my own, who are saying one thing and yet they believe something else."

"But remember," replies Prof. Tracy, "until they entered their seminary studies, they most likely believed the Christian stories and doctrines just as you have. It was only after they were exposed to the critical examination of the Christian religion that they began to understand it differently. And that new knowledge was, I'm sure from my experiences, just as devastating to them as it is to you today.

"And a major part of the dilemma they face in their pastoral life is due to the fact that their seminary experience does not teach nor prepare them in any way to help others, like yourself, to make that leap from Popular Christianity to Academic Christianity.

"Any more questions, comments? If not, let me close out this evening with the final statement from the researchers of this study."

These are brave individuals who are still trying to figure out how to live with the decisions they made many years ago, when they decided, full of devotion and hope, to give their lives to a God they no longer find by their sides. We hope that by telling their stories we will help them and others find more wholehearted ways of doing the good they set out to do. Perhaps the best thing their congregations can do to help them is to respect their unspoken vows of secrecy, and allow them to carry on unchallenged; or perhaps this is a short-sighted response, ultimately just perpetuating the tightly interlocking system that maintains the gulf of systematic hypocrisy between clergy and laity.

"My opinion, of course, is that the unchallenged secrecy they speak of is one of the primary reasons for the decline of the church today.

"And with that we will end this session. Sorry we ran over a bit on the time, but hopefully you got something out of it. Goodnight everybody, see you next week."

15

The Struggle

The group decided they needed to meet separate from Prof. Tracy and sort through some of the emotions that had surfaced during the last meeting. The decision was made to gather for an hour or so Saturday morning at Michel Student Hall. Carol Burke would arrange to reserve a small conference room from 10:00 to 11:00 a.m.

—)(—

"Since I was the one who mouthed off and started the discussion during the meeting the other night, I'll start," said Ted. "I didn't mean anything by my comments. I just thought it was strange how every doctrine we talked about turned out to be a man-made . . . whatever. I'm really sorry it upset some of you."

"I don't think it was so much what you said, Ted," said Helen, "but the realization that what you said pointed out that everything we've ever been taught about the Church seems to be melting away. Everything!"

"I feel responsible," said Lea.

"Responsible for what?" said Jon, "For wanting to learn about Christianity? I'm glad you did, and I'm glad it led to this group. If it hadn't, I might have gone my whole life not knowing the truth about many of the things Prof. Tracy has taught us."

"Maybe we would be better off not knowing," said Greg.

"Are you kidding?" replied Jon. "Religion is—or should be—one of the most important aspects of a person's life. I, for one, want to know all there is to know about the things I believe in. Knowing only half the story leads to half-assed decisions."

Vince interrupts, "Okay, I've had a little extra time on my hands since Wednesday night and I've made a list of the things Prof. Tracy has talked about."

He lays a sheet of paper on the table.

"First he talked about the concept of God.

"Then he talked about Jesus as Savior, or as he called it the Savior Motif.

"Next was the Bible as the word of God, or not.

"Then came Prayer,

"Then the subject of miracles,

"Followed by original sin,

"Then Atonement and the Trinity."

Maria chimed in, "And in every case he stood our personal belief systems on end!"

"Sure, but that doesn't mean we have to buy into everything he's said," replied Greg."

"True, but let me tell you what else I uncovered." continued Vince, "Right here on campus, in our library, you can find books authored by reputable Christian scholars that support every issue Prof. Tracy has brought up. He's not just spouting his opinion, this is knowledge that many Church leaders—the ones not afraid to speak up—have written about for decades.

"Sure, like most of you guys, I'm struggling with some of what we've learned, but I consider myself fortunate to have discovered these things now and not fifty years from now."

"I guess I agree with what you're saying, Vince, but I still feel like I've lost something, like something has been taken away from me." said Helen.

"So, Vince, does that mean that now that you know about these things you're going to leave the church?" asked Carol.

"Well, that brings up a good question," answers Vince, "like, can you *not* believe in God or Jesus as Savior or all those other things, and still be a Christian?"

"Depends," said Ted.

"Depends on what?" asked Vince.

"I would say it depends on whether you feel that being a Christian means believing in all those man-made creeds and stuff of the fourth and fifth century, or you feel that being Christian means trying to live your life as Jesus taught," answered Ted.

"Ted, you are the least religious of all of us, yet you seem to have such clear insight into these things. How come?" said Greg.

"I don't know, maybe it's because I'm more flexible than some of you. Maybe you're too deep in the forest to see the trees, so to speak."

"You may be right," said Maria, "I like your question about what is Christianity, believing in a bunch of man-made propositions, or living your life with love and compassion for others."

"Well, I for one, think it's about living your life with love and compassion for others," said Carol. "But there are a lot of people who would not agree with that idea!"

"Here's another question for you to ponder," said Vince, "If people around the world continue to become more and more educated about these things, will there even be a church in another fifty years?"

"Good question," said Ted. "But can we stay with the discussion about how this new knowledge is affecting us? Let's save the 'Will there be a church?' question 'til later."

"It's hard to just suddenly hear information that dispels beliefs you've held all your life and simply let go and change your mind about what you believe," said Jon.

"On the other hand," said Maria, "if the new information is well founded and accepted by the 'professionals' on the subject, it seems to me one would be foolish not to consider it."

"Or at least do more research," added Carol.

"I think that's the key." said Ted, "So many people will hear these things Prof. Tracy is exposing us to and simply turn away rather than look into them further as some of us have done."

"Even so," said Greg, "it's a hard choice to make. I've talked to two pastors about these things and I've researched some of it and it's still hard to let go."

"Sure," replied Ted. "but in the end doesn't it come down to continuing to believe in ancient superstition and folklore, or accepting twenty-first century knowledge?"

"Yes, Ted, it is," answered Helen, "but it's still a very emotional situation. One that can tear at the very fabric of your soul."

"I can accept that," said Ted. "Yet in the final analysis, isn't it still a decision of whether to believe in superstition and folklore or knowledge?"

"I guess so," said Helen.

"Then how does one bridge that emotional gap? How does a person get past the point of hanging on to the old, let's say for sentimental reasons, and move forward to the more mature position of a knowledge-based understanding?"

"I don't have an answer for that, Ted. Maybe someone else does, but I don't."

They sat in silence for a few moments.

Then Lea spoke, "I guess you could say I am coming into this situation from a neutral position because I haven't heard either the old or the new thoughts before. I can certainly tell you, from my point of view, hearing them for the first time with no preconceived notions, the new knowledge-based explanations are truly the only ones that make sense. That being said, I can certainly understand a person who has heard the old stories for years and years having a hard time looking at the two positions objectively."

"Sorta gets back to what you said earlier, Helen. It makes you feel like everything is melting away, huh?" said Ted

"Yeah, yeah, it really does," replied Helen.

Jon said, "But the teachings of Jesus remain solidly in place!"

16

The Second Coming and Life After Death

When the group entered the meeting room on the next Wednesday evening, Prof. Tracy had the following slide already on the board:

The Second Coming	
Popular Christianity (as understood by people in the pews)	**Academic Christianity** (taught in colleges and seminaries)
Many Christians believe that Jesus ascended into heaven at the completion of his mortal ministry, and two angels declared to his apostles, "This same Jesus, which is taken up from you into heaven, shall soon come in like manner as ye have seen him go into heaven." (Acts 1:11). Since that time, believers have looked forward to the 'second coming' of Jesus Christ.	This idea of the Second Coming of Jesus—known in theological circles as the Parousia—is a human-made concept. It is part of the messianic prophecy, which declares Jesus to be the Son of God. It was developed in the post-Easter era of the developing Church. It has no basis in reality.

Table 10

"I have to leave a little early tonight, so let's jump right into the first topic," said Prof. Tracy, "which I'm sure you've all figured out by now is the Second Coming of Jesus.

"The idea of Jesus' return to Earth, or what most Christians call 'the Second Coming,' is mentioned several times in the New Testament of the Bible—although it is not called the Second Coming. Christian doctrine stresses again and again that followers of 'the Way,' meaning the followers of the teachings of Jesus, should be ever vigilant and prepared for his coming again. The New Testament also describes how his coming may happen at any time, even when we least expect it. Even today, many Christians anticipate the imminent arrival of Christ and look forward to his second coming.

"In the first few years of the early Christian church there were many who lived in a state of expectation that the end may soon be upon them. They believed that Jesus would return to earth at any moment. But as time went on and he did not appear, the idea of the second coming began to fade. Although there were many predictions of his return—which of course did not come true—followers began to become skeptical.

"In the late fourth century St. Augustine, whom we talked about earlier as having written about the idea of Original Sin, began to promote the acceptance of such things as the Second Coming, and the end times, as symbolic or figurative rather than predictions of actual future events. These ideas became quite popular until after the Christian Reformation in the sixteenth century. Prior to that time, the reading and interpretation of the Bible was primarily the domain of the church officials, but now, with the aid of the Gutenberg printing press, the ordinary layman could read the scriptures and form his or her own interpretation, and many chose once again to believe that the scriptures were a foretelling of actual future events.

Helen raised her hand, "At my Baptist church we're reminded every Sunday that Jesus is coming soon and we must be prepared."

"And what does being prepared mean?" asked Prof. Tracy.

"Well, I guess it means living according to the teachings of Jesus and obeying the ten commandments and believing that Jesus is the Son of God, the Savior of the world and things like that."

"Do the things we have discussed in this class interfere with your believing certain things required for being prepared, so to speak?"

"Of course," replied Helen.

"How do you feel about that?" he ask.

"I'm struggling with it."

"Is anyone else struggling?"

All but Lea and Ted raised their hand.

"I'm not surprised," said Prof. Tracy. "You've been exposed to a lot of information in the past few weeks that I'm sure has torn away at the foundation of what you were taught about religion. You need time to process that information. Don't rush it. As time permits, read some books on the subjects we've talked about. I'll try to bring you a list next week of some of my recommendations. For now, let's get back to today's subject, the Second Coming."

He continued with his lecture, "In the nineteenth century an Englishman named John Nelson Darby (1800–1882) invented his own twist on the idea of the Second Coming. In his version, Jesus would appear in the sky and take all the good Christians who had been baptized to a safe place. He called it 'The Rapture.' Then Jesus would supposedly destroy and rebuild the earth and return the Christians to a happy and prosperous life. Many Christian denominations—primarily Evangelicals and Pentecostals—still preach and teach Darby's invented prophecies of the Second Coming of Jesus.

"In all of this, one must keep in mind that the whole idea of the Second Coming of Jesus is inextricably linked to the human concept of God as a supernatural being. Once the supernatural God idea is understood for what it is, the Second Coming becomes nonsensical. In my opinion, the Church ought to admit that the idea of the Second Coming is ancient folklore and has not been taught, in reputable seminaries as a valid concept for decades"

"Do you really see that as a possibility?" asked Jon.

"Well, certainly not soon and not in a universal way. Most likely all of the information we have talked about will be spread by small study groups and individual pastors with the courage and desire to educate their congregations. Tough job."

Looking at his watch, Prof. Tracy says, "I think we have just enough time left this evening for me to introduce you to the final section of doctrine of this series and that is life after death. Perhaps not a subject you want to talk about, but certainly one that comes into view in light of other doctrine we have discussed.

Life After Death	
Popular Christianity (as understood by people in the pews)	**Academic Christianity** (taught in colleges and seminaries)
If a Christian believes that Jesus is the Son of the living God and repents of his or her sins, then, when they die, they will be taken to heaven to live for eternity. Those who do not believe and do not repent will spend eternity in hell.	The concept of a life after death based on a reward/punishment philosophy existed prior to the forming of Christianity. It is a behavior-control tool used to control the masses and provide hope in the face of finite mortality. There is no literal heaven or hell into which humans ascend or descend after death.

Table 11

"I suspect the statement listed under Popular Christianity is basic to what all of you, with the exception of Ms Wong, have been taught by your parents, your church and even society, since your earliest memories. Am I correct?"

Everyone nodded.

"Lea," asked Carol, "what do the Buddhists teach about life after death?"

"Well, Buddhists don't exactly believe in life after death," said Lea. "We believe that this life is temporary. But our spirit lives on after our body dies and returns to this life in some other form, based on how we have lived this current life. And that process continues life after life until we live such a perfect life that we reach what is called Nirvana or enlightenment. I'm probably not explaining it very well, it's kinda complicated."

"I think you did a pretty good job," said Prof. Tracy. "Every religion has its own version of what happens after death, which, of course, adds to the validity of the fact that they are all human ideas—all human ideas, not some, *all*."

Prof. Tracy continues. "In his book, *The Evolution of the Idea of God*, Grant Allen informs us that the idea of an afterlife can be seen in the earliest of religions. In fact, he states that evidence from archeological excavations suggests that humans believed in some kind of life after death long before we began to form religious notions.[14]

"The earliest recorded concepts regarding death and afterlife come from Persia, Egypt, and later Greece. It is thought that the early beliefs of the ancient Israelites about life after death were derived from Middle Eastern cultures. Later Jewish beliefs concerning heaven and hell may have incorporated ideas from the Zoroastrian religion of Persia and the Greek cultures.

"According to historian and sociologist Harry E. Barnes, the earliest ideas of afterlife probably began with the concept known as animism which we talked about earlier. This idea is basically defined as the belief in immortality of one's spiritual self continuing to exist after physical life. Barnes suggests the creation of the supernatural being and the idea of an afterlife were actually originated by man himself as opposed to an almighty being that created life. In other words, the idea of entering into another life after death came about from the ideas and needs of man. [15]

"Perhaps Sigmund Freud in his book, *The Future of an Illusion*, put it most succinctly when he said that belief in the afterlife can be safely dismissed because it is simply a case of human wish fulfillment. He basically said that humans have a juvenile desire to survive death, so we made up the idea of an afterlife.[16]

"As difficult as it will be for Christians—or people of any religion for that matter—to hear the truth, there is simply no rational reason to believe that any form of life or existence continues after the demise of our earthly body."

"Ya know, this is probably the most crushing piece of information you have told us so far," said Maria. "I mean, without a life after death, what's the purpose?"

---

[14] Allen, *Evolution*, 23-32

[15] Barnes, *An Intellectual*, 3rd rev. ed. Vol. 1, 46

[16] Freud, *The Future of an Illusion*, 38-42

"What's the purpose?" Ted said excitedly. "Life here and now, that's the purpose."

Greg chimed in, "But what purpose can there be if this life is all there is?"

"Frankly speaking," said Prof. Tracy, "with or without an afterlife, there is no stated 'purpose' for life. Life is simply something that has occurred on this planet and we are a part of that life. Anything we would call 'purpose' is just something we ourselves have attached to life. The universe is totally benign regarding purpose. That being said, we can each decide for our self what we wish our life to stand for, what we want to be remembered for. We can decide to live a life that benefits others, or we can live a life of thoughtless self-indulgence.

"Throughout history, religions have been a tool used to lead and persuade people to live a life of love, compassion, justice and kindness toward others. Unfortunately, much of the persuasion revolved around fear. Fear of an afterlife of pain and agony. An afterlife that consisted of reward and punishment was effective when most people of the masses were illiterate, but in today's world, one that is much more educated than the world of even fifty or one hundred years ago, that ploy isn't working so well. A more educated populace is more prone to have doubts, ask questions, demand proof or evidence for a doctrine like life after death."

"Isn't that true for all of the doctrines you have discussed with us?" asked Carol.

"Yes, it is," answered Prof. Tracy.

"So, does that mean that as our society becomes more and more educated Christianity will slowly fade and disappear?" asked Greg.

"I doubt it will disappear," said Prof. Tracy. "Rather, I think its current form will become smaller and smaller. In its place, in the mainstream of society, I believe we will see many new expressions of Christianity and spirituality.

"Even today there are hundreds, perhaps thousands of small gatherings of Christians taking place each week in private homes where religion is studied and discussed. People are opting out of the institutional church with its ancient belief systems and creeds and moving toward a more reality-based spirituality of love and care for others. The movement seems to be back to living the teachings of Jesus that are associated with the early church, before the addition of the mythology and creeds of the fourth and fifth century.

"Okay, that will do it for tonight. Next week we will discuss the Synoptic Gospels. I can assure you, you will be surprised at what I have in store for you."

17

The Synoptic Gospels

The group assembled for their Wednesday evening meeting, without Vince Morgan. Ted informed the group that Vince had texted that he would be a little bit late. Something about a job interview.

"Well," began Prof. Tracy. "This session may be a bit longer than usual, but I can almost promise it will be mind boggling. You will learn something tonight that has always been right before your eyes as you read the Gospels, but you have never seen it. Something that will change the way you look at the New Testament forever!"

"Wow," said Ted excitedly. "I'm all in, let's go!"

The entire group seemed to snap to attention in anticipation.

"Okay then, here we go." said Prof. Tracy. "The first thing we have to remember as we begin this session is that Jesus was a Jew. He grew up in a Jewish family and he never left the Jewish faith."

"But I thought he started the Christian church," said Helen.

"No no, Jesus was a reformer. He wanted to reform the Jewish faith. His disciples were all Jewish. The movement we call Christianity, actually began and resided within the Jewish synagogue for more than fifty years after Jesus' death before it split and became a separate entity. After Jesus death those who continued to follow his teachings were called 'followers of The Way.'

"Okay, moving along. . . . For starters, let me introduce you to the structure of the synagogue worship service as it was practiced in the first century and is still practiced in many synagogues today.

"The first five books of what we call the Old Testament are known to the Jews as the Torah—Genesis, Exodus, Leviticus, Numbers, and Deuteronomy. The Torah is considered to be the law of God as revealed by God to Moses. As a part of the Jewish worship service, held each Sabbath day, a portion of the Torah is read aloud to the congregation, so that over the course of one year, the entire five books of the Torah are read. Then the process starts over again.

"Each Sabbath, after the reading of the appropriate portion of the Torah, there might be a reading from one of the Prophets or one of the Psalms. Then there would be a time for members of the congregation to speak and tell stories that related to the Torah reading of the day. This is the place in the service that the followers of 'the Way' would have an opportunity to tell stories of Jesus. Their purpose was to liken Jesus to the Jewish heroes of the past—Moses, Elijah, Elisa, Joshua.

"I tell you these things to prepare you for our study of the Synoptics." Prof. Tracy paused to put the following slide on the board. (Table 12 next page)

"Prof. Tracy, what does Synoptic mean?" asked Carol.

"The word Synoptic used this way means, 'similar in content.' You'll see that as we move ahead, and remember, all of this information can be found in your Bible.

"Take a look at this slide," he said. "It depicts the major holidays and celebrations of the Jewish faith. Remember now, the Torah is being read in the Temple on a yearly basis; therefore there are readings in the Torah that are read and reflected upon during each of these holidays.

"Let me take a moment to briefly explain each of them.

"Rosh Hashanah is the Jewish New Year. You will notice on the slide, it occurs in late September of our calendar. It is observed in the Jewish tradition with prayers for the coming of the Kingdom of God and a call to repentance.

"Next comes Yom Kippur. It occurs ten days after Rosh

Synoptic Gospels Patterned After Torah			
	Torah	**Mark**	**Matthew**	**Luke**
Jan				
Feb				
Mar	Passover			
Apl				
May	Shavuot			
June				
Jul				
Aug				
Sept	Rosh Hashanah			
Oct	Yom Kippur			
	Sukkoth			
Nov				
Dec	Hanukkah			

Table 12

Hashanah. This is the Jewish Day of Atonement, a day to ask God to forgive the sins of the people. Sacrifices were offered in the temple during this celebration."

"Isn't that when they used the scapegoat?" asked Helen.

"Yes," answered Prof. Tracy.

"Scapegoat? I don't understand," said Lea.

Prof. Tracy explains, "This was a part of the Atonement process we discussed a few weeks ago. The Priests of the Temple would symbolically place the sins of the people on the back of a goat. The goat was then banished to the desert and the people were thought to be freed from their sins for another year.

"Then came the harvest festival in late October known as Sukkoth. Possibly similar to Thanksgiving in this country. This was an eight day celebration. It was also known as Booths or Tabernacles. It also had a religious significance, commemorating the Jewish Exodus from Egypt and their dependence on the will of God.

"Next in mid December came the holiday Hanukkah. This was a celebration of the rededication of the Temple and the return of God's light to the Temple.

"Then there was a long period during January and February where there were no major celebrations. This dry period ended in late March or early April when the Passover celebration was held. This was a day to remember the time during the Jewish exodus from Egypt when the angel of death passed over the Jewish homes and spared the lives of the first born sons. You remember we talked about that event in an earlier session?"

All nodded affirmatively.

"The last of the major celebrations is called Shavuot. It occurred fifty days after Passover. It was a remembrance or celebration of Moses receiving the laws that govern the Jewish lives, from God on Mount Sinai.

"So, that 'in a nut shell' as they say, is a short description of the Jewish holidays. Now what I'm going to show you is how the Gospels were written to standardize the stories the followers of 'the Way' would tell from Sabbath to Sabbath after the Torah reading. You will see how the Gospel writings line up with the Torah on these special holidays and celebrations.

"First we'll look at the Gospel of Mark—the first of the Gospels, written about the year 70 or 72 CE. Understand, we call this book 'Mark' but scholars have no idea who actually wrote it. Scholars believe it was written from Rome.

"Look now at Mark's writings lined up next to the Jewish holidays.

"I thought all the Gospels were written by disciples of Jesus," said Greg.

"I'm afraid not," answered Prof. Tracy. "The Gospels were written between 70 and 105 CE, which means they were probably written two, or in the case of the book of John, three generations after Jesus lived. No one knows who wrote them. They were given the names, Mark, Matthew, Luke and John sometime in the second century. These are the findings of reputable scholars of today. Still, there are Pastors who will preach that the disciples wrote them because saying so tends to give them more credence.

Synoptic Gospels patterned after Torah			
	Torah	Mark	Matthew	Luke
Jan				
Feb				
Mar	Passover	Crucifixion		
Apl				
May	Shavuot			
June				
Jul				
Aug				
Sept	Rosh Hashanah	John / Baptism		
Oct	Yom Kippur	Healing		
	Sukkoth	Sower		
Nov				
Dec	Hanukkah	Transfiguration		

Table 13

"We start our tour of Mark by looking at Rosh Hashanah, the Jewish New Year. During this celebration a ram's horn is blown—called a shofar—to announce that the Kingdom of God is at hand. Mark begins his Gospel with the story of John the Baptist baptizing Jesus and announcing to the crowd that the Kingdom of God is at hand in Jesus. He uses John the Baptist as a human shofar. A perfect story to complement the meaning and celebration of Rosh Hashanah and it comes to us in Mark Chapter 1:1-11. A clear parallel between Mark and the Torah.

"Now let's move forward to the celebration of Yom Kippur and the day of atonement, forgiveness, and healing. Here in Mark, chapters 2 and 3, we find stories of healing and cleaning, enough for the daily readings of this eight day celebration. Another perfect match.

"Moving now to October to the Jewish holiday of harvest and thanksgiving known as Sukkoth, we find in Mark chapter 4, the story Jesus told of the sower who sows seed on four kinds of soil producing four different results—you remember that story—an obvious harvest theme for this harvest celebration.

"In December we find the holiday called Hanukkah. Held at or near the time of the winter solstice, which marks the shortest day and longest night of the year in the Northern Hemisphere, Hanukkah is a rededication of the Temple and is marked by the successive lighting of eight candles over the eight days of the holiday. It also commemorates the return of God's light to the Temple. It is at this point in Mark chapter 9:2-10 that we find the story of the Transfiguration, where the light of God falls on Jesus, Moses and Elijah. Mark is saying that the light is now falling, not on the Temple, which by now has been destroyed by the Romans, but on Jesus.

"Then after the long period from January to March, we come to the celebration of the Passover.

"In the original story, you'll remember, God instructs the Hebrews to place the blood of a lamb above their door so the angel of death, sent to kill the first born male of the Egyptians, will pass them by and thus save the lives of their first born sons. The Hebrews are later instructed to commemorate this occurrence annually with the sacrifice of a Passover or 'Paschal' lamb. At this point in the Gospel Mark relates the story of Jesus' crucifixion and resurrection, the implication being that Jesus was the new Paschal lamb. That implication relates to Paul's writing some fifteen years earlier, in a letter to the Corinthians that Jesus was the new 'Paschal lamb, who has been sacrificed for us'. We talked about that during an earlier session also.

"It is interesting to note that Mark devotes 40 percent of his Gospel to the story of Jesus' last week of life, and in that story he devotes 105 verses to the events of the crucifixion and only eight verses to the resurrection."

"So, what is the significance of that?" asked Jon.

"I'm not sure," answered Prof. Tracy, "but it seems a bit odd, since in church history the emphasis is mostly on the resurrection. Bishop Spong makes this statement in his book, *Re-Claiming the Bible for a Non-Religious World.*

Mark's story of the crucifixion is not remembered history, it is a second-generation interpretation of Jesus death, shaped by Jewish messianic expectations through the ages.[17]

"In fact, none of Mark's Gospel is history; it is, as we have just seen, liturgy crafted to relate Jesus stories to synagogue worship for the six and a half month period from Rosh Hashanah to Passover.

"I always thought the Gospels were sort of a biography of Jesus' life." said Helen.

"Let me point out a few more examples that will hopefully help you see Mark as interpretive liturgy instead of biographical history," said Prof. Tracy. "I'm going to assume that most of you, except Ms Wong, have read or heard the crucifixion story in Mark. Many of the words and visual descriptions from that story came from Psalm 22 and Isaiah 53, in the Old Testament. Remember Mark saying that Jesus cried out from the cross, 'My God, my God, why have you forsaken me?'. Those words are a direct quote from Psalm 22:1. Those words were written about King David who lived one thousand years before Jesus. All of Psalm 22 was written about King David.

"Mark later has one of the Roman soldiers say, 'Since he trusted in God, let God deliver him.' This is a quote of verse eight of Psalm 22.

"He later implies that Jesus is thirsty, this comes from verse 15.

"The piercing of Jesus' feet and hands comes from verse 16.

"The casting of lots for Jesus' robe comes from verse 18.

"Are you starting to get the picture?

"Mark also uses word images he finds in Isaiah 53: the 'suffering servant', 'wounded for our transgressions', 'bruised for our iniquities', 'with his stripes we are healed'. All the while Mark is building an

---

[17] Spong, *Re-Claiming the Bible*, 312

interpretive memory to be used as liturgy."

"Wow," said Ted, "certainly is a different way of looking at the Gospel!"

"And yet it's always been there, right in front of us," said Prof. Tracy. "But because we are not Jewish and therefore not intimately knowledgeable about the Torah or the Old Testament, we don't see the connection. The Jewish worshipers of the first century would have understood with little or no effort.

"It gets even more interesting; let's move on now to the Gospel called Matthew.

Synoptic Gospels patterned after Torah			
	Torah	Mark	Matthew	Luke
Jan				
Feb				
Mar	Passover	Crucifixion	Same as Mark	
Apl				
May	Shavuot		Sermon on Mount	
			Genealogy	
June			Birth Story	
Jul			Joseph Story	
			Baptism Story	
Aug			Temptations	
Sept	Rosh Hashanah	John / Baptism	John / Prison	
Oct	Yom Kippur	Healing	Same as Mark	
	Sukkoth	Sower	Same as Mark	
Nov				
Dec	Hanukkah	Transfiguration	Same as Mark	

Table 14

"The book we call Matthew is thought to have been written in Antioch, Syria around the years 82 to 85.

"The writer incorporates about 80 percent of the writings of Mark and uses the same structure as Mark. Bishop Spong calls Matthew 'the most Jewish' of the gospels. Matthew contains several stories that we haven't heard in Mark: the virgin birth story, the story of the magi following the star, King Herod sending soldiers to slaughter Jewish boy babies, Joseph fleeing with Mary and Jesus to Egypt, and Joseph having a dream telling him to take Jesus to grow up in Galilee.

"Why do you suppose he wrote those additional stories?" asked Prof. Tracy.

"Well," said Maria, "looking at the slide, I would say he wrote them to fill in the part of the year where Mark had no stories."

"You are correct," replied Prof. Tracy. "There must have been those who felt they needed liturgy for the whole year, not just the six and a half months that Mark covered, so Matthew took care of that situation. In doing so he also attempts to accomplish some other goals.

"He begins his Gospel with a genealogy of Jesus that is intended to show that Jesus is not only a direct descendent of King David but also a descendent of Abraham, the father of Judaism. When we get to Luke you will find that he also wrote a genealogy; however, he takes Jesus' lineage all the way back to Adam and Eve! Of course as you might suspect, scholars don't believe either of the genealogies are correct; in fact, the two of them don't even agree with each other.

"Next Matthew brings us his birth story. I say 'his' because the birth story in Luke, the only other birth story in the Bible, is quite different.

"In Matthew's birth story we meet Jesus' parents, Mary and Joseph.

"Matthew must have also had a desire to bring a closer relationship between the Jews who lived in the region of Judah, who identified primarily with their ancestor King David, and the Jews of the Northern Kingdom whose primary ancestor was Joseph of the Old Testament. He had already associated Jesus with the people of Judah by showing his genealogical connection to King David. But how would he associate him with Joseph of the Old Testament? Well, here's what he did. . . . remember the story of Joseph in the Old Testament? Joseph was the youngest son of Jacob."

"Joseph and the coat of many colors," said Jon.

"That's the one," said Prof. Tracy. "As the story goes, Joseph was Jacob's favorite son and Joseph's brothers were jealous of him. One thing leads to another and the brothers end up selling Joseph to a Middianite merchant who took him down to Egypt and sold him to one of the Pharaoh's officials. Time moves on and Joseph becomes an interpreter of dreams and lands a very important job in the Pharaoh's government, in charge of all the land and grain of Egypt.

"A great famine comes to Canaan where Joseph's brothers are living and, fast forward, he allows them and their families to come to Egypt to live to prevent them from starving. Now, with that background, here's how Matthew ties Joseph to Jesus: First he gives Jesus a father named, you guessed it, Joseph. And in Matthew 1:16 we discover that Joseph's father is named. . . . Jacob. The Joseph of the Old Testament is associated with dreams, and how does Joseph of the New Testament find out about Mary's pregnancy? In a dream. Later he has a dream where God supposedly tells him to take Mary and Jesus and go to Egypt to save Jesus from the evil King Herod. So the Old Testament Joseph took the Hebrews to Egypt to save their lives, and the New Testament Joseph takes Jesus to Egypt to save his life.

"So there we have it, old Joseph and new Joseph, both have fathers named Jacob, old and new, both known for dreams, old and new, both saved lives by taking folks to Egypt.

"Now the North and the South are both represented in the Jesus story. Convenient, huh?"

"I never noticed that before now," said Carol.

"Of course not, because you're not Jewish!" said Prof. Tracy.

They all chuckled.

"Now Matthew moves to the story of John the Baptist baptizing Jesus, but he has to tell it earlier than Mark did because he still has several weeks to cover before he gets to Rosh Hashanah.

"After his baptism, you will remember, Jesus went into the desert and was challenged by the devil. Here Matthew makes another comparison, this time between Jesus and Moses.

"The first test or challenge Moses faced was lack of food for the Hebrew people. This was satisfied with manna from heaven. The first test the devil placed before Jesus was, 'Change these rocks to bread.'

"Later Moses tested God by striking a rock with his staff and asking for water to flow from it. The devil challenged Jesus to test God by throwing himself off a cliff and asking God to save him.

"In a third test Moses came down from Mount Sinai and found the people worshiping an idol. The devil likewise tested Jesus saying, 'Bow down before me and I will give you the world.'

"So, Matthew has given us another comparison between the Old and New Testament. He is making Jesus the new Moses. It is a form of ancient Rabbinic writing called Midrash. Any questions?"

No one said anything.

"Okay then, we have now come to Rosh Hashanah and now Matthew writes another John the Baptist story. This time John is in prison.

"Then Matthew copies Mark for the next four holidays—Yom Kippur, Sukkoth, Hanukkah and Passover.

Ted exclaimed, "Amazing, this answers so many questions at so many levels. Suddenly I'm starting to understand the purpose and meaning of the Gospels like never before."

"Yes, me too," said Helen, "but I'm not sure I like it."

"Why not?" asked Greg.

"Because, like I said before, it destroys so much of what I learned as a child."

"And that's a natural reaction, Helen," said Prof. Tracy. "That anxious feeling will fade as you absorb more information."

Prof. Tracy continued his presentation.

"You will notice on the slide, Mark had not written scripture for use at the holiday of Shavuot, which commemorated the time when, on Mount Sinai, God supposedly gave Moses 'the law' which governs the lives of the Hebrew people. Matthew chose to close that gap.

"Shavuot is a twenty-four hour celebration during which, in the Jewish tradition, Psalm 119 is read. Psalm 119 is the longest of the Psalms. It begins with eight short verses, followed by eight sections, one pertaining to each of the opening verses. One of these eight sections was read during each of the three hour segments of the twenty-four hour Shavuot celebration.

"So what did Matthew do for this occasion? Well, in like manner, he begins his writing with eight short verses, just as in Psalm 119, then he writes eight sections, one for each verse, again the same as Psalm 119. Some scholars believe these sections were written around oral tradition and other collections of sayings attributed to Jesus.

"The first two verses of the eight verses that begin Psalm 119 begin with the word 'Blessed'. Matthew began *all eight verses* of his writing with 'Blessed'. We call these eight verses the Beatitudes. We call this whole section of Matthew, Chapters 5-6-7, the Sermon on the Mount.

"Matthew has now provided material for the twenty-four hours of Shavuot and he has succeeded in providing commentary for the entire year of synagogue worship."

"So, you're saying that the Sermon on the Mount came from Matthew, not Jesus?" asked Jon.

"It came from the writer of Matthew, whoever he was. Yes, that's right," said Prof. Tracy. "And let me remind you again, these writers were not writing history, they were writing stories to be read in the synagogue in conjunction with the Torah stories on each Sabbath of the year."

Prof. Tracy looked around the room; everyone seemed restless. "Let's take a short break and then we'll come back and finish up with Luke. See you back here in ten minutes."

Greg and Lea stepped outside the front doors of Westlake Hall, into the cool night air.

"How are you taking this?" asked Lea.

"Well, I'm surprised but I'm okay with it. I guess I'm surprised because it has always been there and I've never seen it and no one has ever mentioned it before."

"Yeah, I suppose it would come as a surprise when you think of it having always been there. But like Prof. Tracy said, 'You're not Jewish!' Maybe if you were you'd have noticed the pattern."

"I suppose so."

Vince, who had arrived shortly after the lecture began, walks over to where they are standing, "Boy, this is interesting information. Seems so much more logical when you see it this way. I can't count how many times I've read parts of the Gospels, but this puts a really different light on them."

"Yeah," said Greg, "we were just saying the same thing."

"I know, early on, you were having trouble with the things Prof. Tracy was teaching us. Are you becoming more comfortable with the class now?" asked Vince.

"I guess so. I had quite a resistance for awhile, but it's starting to make sense now. Don't know if I would say I'm fully convinced, but there isn't much room for argument when you start reading the history of some of these things."

"We better get back inside," said Lea.

Prof. Tracy began, "The Gospel of Luke is thought to have been written sometime in the late 80's or early 90's of the first century. The writer of Luke also wrote the Book of Acts. It is believed that the writer might have been a Gentile who had converted to Judaism. He may have been one of Paul's converts. Most scholars say that he wrote from Ephesus in Asia Minor.

"Luke uses the same overall structure as Mark and Matthew. He makes very little change to the storyline, except when he get to Shavuot and Yom Kippur. I'll talk about that later. Luke copies about sixty percent of Mark.

"There are some stories in Luke that do not appear in Mark, but do appear in Matthew. This has led many scholars to hypothesize that Matthew and Luke used another document for some of their writings. They refer to this unknown document as the 'Q' document. No copy of the 'Q' has ever been found. A minority of scholars feel that Luke may have had both Mark and Matthew in front of him when he was writing and simply copied some of the stories Matthew had written that do not appear in Mark.

"Although the details of the stories vary to some degree, Luke uses the same theme as Matthew for the celebration of Passover, and the filler material for the birth story and the baptism story. He copies

Mark for Rosh Hashanah, Sukkoth and Hanukkah. However, for Yom Kippur, he inserts the story of the woman washing Jesus' feet with her tears and drying them with her hair. To make this a cleansing story, Luke has Jesus forgive the woman of her sins in a clear reference to the Yom Kippur theme.

Synoptic Gospels patterned after Torah			
Torah	Mark	Matthew	Luke
Jan			
Feb			
Mar	Passover	Crucifixion	Same as Mark	Same as Matthew
Apl			
May	Shavuot		Sermon on Mount	Ascension/Holy Spirit
			Genealogy	
June			Birth Story	Sim. to Matthew
Jul			Joseph Story	
			Baptism Story	Same as Matthew
Aug			Temptations	
Sept	RoshHashanah	John/Baptism	John / Prison	Same as Mark
Oct	Yom Kippur	Healing	Same as Mark	Woman wash feet
	Sukkoth	Sower	Same as Mark	Same as Mark
Nov				
Dec	Hanukkah	Transfiguration	Same as Mark	Same as Mark

Table 15

"Luke was the first to tell of angels singing at Jesus' birth. He is the only one of the three that tells the story of Jesus raising the dead son of a widow in the village on Nain, very similar to a story in I Kings where Elijah was said to have raised the son of a widow. Luke seems to be comparing Jesus to Elijah in this story.

"The Gospel of Luke is the only place we read the parable of the Good Samaritan. This would be important to the writer of Luke if indeed he were a Gentile.

"In a major departure from Mark and Matthew, Luke, in the book of Acts, Chapter 1, tells a story of the ascension of Jesus into heaven. He places the story at the time of the year of the Shavuot celebration. It becomes another attempt to compare Jesus to Elijah.

You might recall that in II Kings, Chapter 2 there is a story of Elijah ascending to heaven riding in a fiery chariot. Well, in Luke's story, Jesus doesn't need a chariot, he ascends under his own power. But Luke takes the fire from Elijah's chariot and turns it into 'tongues of fire' that dance on the heads of all the followers of Jesus who have gathered at what we Christians call Pentecost. He takes the whirlwind that propelled Elijah's chariot heavenward and turns it into a 'mighty rushing wind' that filled the room where the people were gathered.

"Now Luke's Gospel fills the entire year of synagogue life, the same as Matthew.

"So, let me make a quick summery. The Synoptic Gospels were written some forty to sixty years after Jesus' death by writers who never met Jesus, did not know him, never heard him speak. The structure of all three suggest they were meant to be read in the Synagogue in conjunction with the reading of the Torah. They are not historical accounts of the life of Jesus. They are valuable to our faith tradition, but need to be understood properly."

Prof. Tracy paused and looked around the room at the faces of the students. He was somewhat sad that the class was nearing its end. These young people seemed truly interested in what he was teaching them each and every week. They were there because they wanted to be there, not because they had to earn a credit.

"Okay, that will do it for tonight. I would like to have one more meeting with you to critique what you have gotten out of the class, and answer any unanswered questions you might have. See you next week."

As the group exited Westlake Hall, Ted said, "I think we ought to get together Sunday afternoon and prepare a list of things we want to ask, so we don't all get there and basically all ask the same questions."

They agreed to meet at the Michel Student Center at 2:30 p.m. on Sunday.

18

Final Session

Rain and sleet filled the skies on Wednesday evening. It was cold, a good night for a fireplace and a book. As Prof. Tracy made his way to the meeting room he wondered how many, if any, of the group would show up. Much to his surprise, when he entered the room everyone was already there, including Ted who had been habitually late for most of the prior meetings.

"Well, said Prof. Tracy, "this is interesting! Last class of the series and everyone eager to get started. Hope I can interpret that to mean you've enjoyed the sessions."

"I'd have to say I've enjoyed the sessions but I've also been very perplexed by them," replied Helen.

"That's understandable, Helen," said Prof. Tracy. "No one would expect you to feel any other way. We have been discussing some very important subjects that are very meaningful to most people. It will take time and additional study to bring you fully convinced into this new understanding of religion."

Greg spoke up, "I guess, for me, the crux of the whole idea of a new way to understand religion, or Christianity, is the issue of God. If the God of the Bible doesn't exist then I have no problem with the Trinity or the virgin birth or any of the other stuff not being true. But it's a really big, big step to say there's no God, that's my hang-up."

"And that's exactly why I brought up the issue of the concept of God in our first session. It has relevance to all the other elements of the study." said Prof. Tracy.

"I thought you told us you talked to a couple of pastors and they agreed with the stuff we've learned here, about God," said Maria, speaking to Greg.

"Yes, I did," replied Greg. "But I'm still reluctant to just roll over and say there's no God."

"What would convince you?" asked Ted.

"I don't know," said Greg.

"When I spoke of God in our earlier session," said Prof. Tracy, "I explained how our earliest ancestors imagined that gods or spirits were at the root of all the mysteries of nature. Things like the sun, rain, wind, flowing rivers and streams, and so much more, were all controlled by these imagined gods or spirits. Then we talked about how those gods and spirits changed over time, becoming human-like, taking on personalities, how the people worshiped and sacrificed to them in order to seek favor. Down through the ages, over thousands of years, various gods have come and gone as new ones are imagined and old ones are discarded. Today there are roughly a thousand gods and goddesses worshiped around the world, and every one of them is simply a modern day manifestation of those ancient gods of our forefathers. They are imaginary. They are figments of our human mind. Ask yourself . . . where else could they have come from?"

Jon said, "I want to say, 'Yes, *but*,'. . . . but it really all makes sense when you allow yourself to look at history objectively and rationally."

"The problem," replied Prof. Tracy, "stems from the fact that most of us were taught about God at an early age. An age before our minds were able to see things objectively or rationally. In that situation we accept the idea of a Father God, protector, helper, judge, without question, as a core value of how the world works. We accept it because someone we looked up to, our mother, father, Sunday school teacher, told us so. Later in life, when we could think objectively and rationally, it became extremely hard for us to ever re-examine or re-think those core values. Some people simply never can and never will."

"I think my problem is: I believe what you're saying but I'm not ready yet to give up my comfortable Father God, protector, helper, judge." said Greg.

"I fully understand," said Prof. Tracy.

"Reminds me of a little poem from the movie Heartless," said Vince,

Lie to me just a little bit longer,
Lie to me 'til I'm a little bit stronger,
I'm not ready yet,
to accept the truth,
so . . . lie to me.

"Wow, said Ted, "I like that, it says a lot. Write that down for me!"

"It still seems like everything we have learned in this class has been geared to destroy Christianity and the church," said Helen.

"What a perfect segue!" said Prof. Tracy, "I was about to begin my closing remarks and your comment gives me a perfect entry point. You're right, Helen, everything we have talked about has *deconstructed* the Christian faith. From the concept of God to the stories of Jesus' birth, his miracles, the atonement and everything else. All seemingly destructive. But as the TV personality Dr. Phil is fond of saying, *'No matter how flat you make a pancake, it still has two sides!'* So let me try to explain both sides of this proverbial pancake and in the process perhaps I can kind of summarize everything we've covered these past several weeks.

"Christian churches in America have been in trouble for several decades. This is no secret. Membership and attendance have been dropping in almost every denomination, revenues have been decreasing, churches have been closing. Depending on which survey you look at, membership in Christianity as a whole has been dropping, on average, about two to two and a half million people per year.

Church closings are exceeding new church starts by 3,000 to 3,500 per year, and clergy are leaving the church in excess of 1,500 a month.

"So more recent surveys have begun to ask the question, 'Why don't you belong to a church? Or, 'Why don't you attend church?' And the most recent surveys by the Pew Research Center are pointing to a greater and greater number of people giving as their number one reason that they do not believe what the church is preaching, teaching, singing and praying. They do not believe what the church seems to believe.[18]

"Well, guess what? Neither do the most reputable scholars and leaders of the church! For many generations, church scholars have known that the doctrines of the church needed to be corrected to match current knowledge of life, of the human condition, of the universe. The items we have discussed in this class are just some of those doctrines. The information I have been presenting to you is not new; most of it is hundreds of years old.

"Then why the heck are the churches not teaching it?" asked Jon.

"Well, we went over that in one of our earlier sessions, Jon, but let me remind you," answered Prof. Tracy. "For the most part of the past 2,000 years the Christian church has occupied a position of power and prestige in human society. This has been true for other religions as well, of course. This power and prestige extended from the local clergy to the highest offices of the institutional church. It has allowed the church to have a great deal of control over the lives of the masses. And, not coincidentally, to extract sufficient revenues from those masses to purchase, build, and support its buildings and facilities, and to pay the salaries of its employees and provide some support to the poor and disenfranchised in its communities. Albeit, a small portion in most cases goes to the latter.

"When this new understanding of church doctrine started to become known among scholars, in the seventeenth and eighteenth

---

[18] PRRI, *www.prri.org/ topic/ religion-culture*

centuries, it seems it was not thought to be in the best interest of the church to make such knowledge known to the masses. The fear seemed to be, and still is, that such knowledge would drive many people away from the church and thus negatively affect the church's influence, control and, perhaps most importantly, revenue. And so, either on purpose or simply by default, this information has not made its way to church pulpits.

"Now, here's the other side of that pancake.

"Sometime around the middle of the twentieth century, a tear appeared in this 'invisible velvet curtain' that was protecting the church. I don't know how or when the first tear occurred, but one of the earliest books I have found on the subject is a little book written in 1962, by Bishop John A.T. Robinson, Bishop of Woolwich, England. The book is titled, *Honest to God*. While the Bishop does not say so in the book, it would appear, from my perspective, that he was writing the book for distribution to officials of the church. However, it somehow made its way to the public domain and sales flourished around the world. It is still a popular seller today and is used in many college courses on religion.

"The Bishop makes this statement in the preface of the book:

. . . .*I believe we are being called, over the years ahead, to far more than a restating of traditional orthodoxy in modern terms. Instead, if our defense of the Faith is limited to this, we shall find in all likelihood that we have lost out to all but a tiny religious remnant. A much more radical recasting, I would judge is demanded, in the process of which the most fundamental categories of our theology—of God, of the supernatural, and of religion itself—must go into the melting.*

Then, further in the book, on page 124, he writes:

What looks like being required of us, reluctant as we may be for the effort involved, is a radically new mould, or metamorphosis, of

Christian belief and practice. Such a recasting will, I am convinced, leave the fundamental truth of the Gospel unaffected. But it means that we have to be prepared for everything to go into the melting—even our most cherished religious categories and moral absolutes. And the first thing we must be ready to let go is our image of God himself.

"You can imagine what an uproar this must have caused both inside and outside the church!"

"What happened to Bishop Robinson?" asked Greg.

"Nothing extraordinary. He remained at Woolwich until 1969 then became Dean of Chapel at Trinity College. He died of cancer in 1983. Of course, controversy still surrounds his book to this day.

"That tear in the 'invisible velvet curtain' however, seemed to create a groundswell of books introducing a more intellectually honest understanding of various areas of church doctrine based on studies that reached back as far as the seventeenth century. And today that curtain has been all but torn away in religious academia. Many colleges and seminaries across the country are teaching a more scholarly and intellectually honest Christianity. A great many of the pastors and priests serving today have been taught the new understandings. Yet it seems that for 99 percent of our churches, the preaching is still floundering with doctrine that is 300 years out of sync with current knowledge. And so, people who read the books that introduce the new understanding, and students of our colleges and seminaries who study the new understandings, are finding the local churches no longer speaking to them. They are finding the church repressive, out of date, and irrelevant, and they are leaving or staying away by the millions. The fastest growing group of people in the spectrum of religious surveys today, are the 'nones', those who say they have no religious affiliation. And it's the continued growth of this group that is contributing to the decline in the membership of our churches.

"Now, here's the other side of the pancake."

"Wait," said Carol. "You've already talked about both sides of the pancake."

"Yes, but I fooled you," Prof, Tracy said, smiling. "This pancake has three sides !"

"Three sides? Really?" exclaimed Ted.

"Yep, three sides," said Prof. Tracy. "Let me explain. If we step back from the world of Christianity a bit, we will see that it is built on two separate platforms, one called orthodoxy the other called orthopraxy."

"Orthopraxy?" said Jon. "I've heard of orthodoxy but what is orthopraxy?"

"Basically orthopraxy speaks to how we as Christians are to conduct ourselves in our daily lives, how we are to relate ethically to the world around us. Orthodoxy, on the other hand, emphasizes what we are to believe and those beliefs come to us primarily from the creeds of the fourth and fifth centuries.

"We can see prime examples of these two platforms in the early writings of the Bible: Paul's epistles tell us that he (Paul) felt that what we believe about God and the life and death and resurrection of Jesus is of utmost importance. The gospels of Mark, Matthew, and Luke, however, tend to tell us how to live our lives through examples revealed in the parables. A couple of centuries later, when the creeds are written, the beliefs, or orthodoxy, took center stage, and how we are to conduct our lives, orthopraxy, tended to become secondary."

"But hasn't the church always practiced compassion for the poor and downtrodden?" asked Helen.

"Yes," replied Prof. Tracy. "But many in the church will tell you, you can be a good person but still go to hell if you don't believe the right things: emphasis on orthodoxy first, orthopraxy second.

"I tell you these things to explain my position concerning the church of the future, or perhaps more properly put, Christianity of the future.

"I maintain that Christianity must reverse its priority and make orthopraxy its primary emphasis. This is critical to the church's survival—again, my opinion. But reversing its priority is not enough; it must 'come clean', update, correct—use whatever words you will—the prevailing understanding of the official doctrine of the church. It must bring its doctrinal knowledge into the 21st century and change its preaching, teaching, singing and praying to reflect this new knowledge as well. To not do so, will contribute to the continued decline of its membership."

"But, Prof. Tracy," said Greg. "Won't that, in itself, cause a drop in membership? Won't people leave the church feeling it is just an empty shell?"

"Quite possibly." said Prof. Tracy, "It's sort of a 'Catch 22' situation for the church. If nothing is changed, the church will continue to decline as it is doing now. If it makes the changes we are talking about, it may well decline in the near term, but in the long term I truly believe it will flourish. I believe the more educated our society becomes, the less it will tolerate an institution that continues to preach folklore and superstition as truth."

"But if the church disavows its doctrine, what will be left?" asked Carol.

"Think back to what I just said about orthodoxy and orthopraxy, Carol. Orthopraxy will not be affected by an update to what we believe. The teachings of Jesus—to love one another, to care for the sick, the poor, the homeless—does not change when we update our knowledge of the concept of God or the Savior Motif or any of the other doctrines we have looked at. What people must come to accept is that the Bible expresses a religious belief system that *was*, not the religious belief system that *is*. The knowledge we have of such things today far exceeds that which was known in the first century. The information we have been studying in this class does not destroy orthodoxy, it takes orthodoxy to a new level of adult maturity. Our churches, in whatever form they take in the future, will need to take this into consideration. However, the way we ought to live our lives— following the teachings of Jesus—has not changed and should, once again, become the core of Christian life. Which brings me to some final thoughts about the church of the future. In my opinion, the church of tomorrow will not be a big brick or limestone building on the corner with large stained glass windows and a huge steeple reaching to the sky. In fact the trend even today is away from the kind of church I just described and toward a more modest facility."

"Well, Prof. Tracy," asked Helen, "does the church have to be in a building? Could it take on some other form?"

"Actually Helen, there are already several alternative situations where people are seeking spirituality today: In home churches where small groups gather to study some of the books I've mentioned; In groups that meet in coffee houses, in bars, in city parks; There are groups that are forming virtual churches online. I suspect the future will bring even more innovation as more and more people seek to excuse themselves from institutional religion but still feel a need to gather in community and to come together to support the poor, the homeless and others in need in our society."

"So Christianity, or the orthopraxy of Christianity, will not go away?" asked Maria.

"Let's hope not," said Prof. Tracy. "Without love and compassion for our fellow human beings, this would be a sorry, sorry world."

Prof. Tracy expressed his thanks to the group for their dedication to the class. They, in turn, thanked him for his giving of his time and for the sharing of knowledge. Lea Wong thanked everyone for participating in the class and stated that she was so very happy to have had such an opportunity to learn and share with everyone.

Class dismissed.

Follow-up: In the weeks to come, Helen, Ted, and Jon formed a study group that included four other friends and began reading Bishop Spong's book, A *New Christianity for a New World*.

Vince, Carol, and Greg introduced their Methodist youth group to some of the information Prof. Tracy had taught them. During the next school year they plan to continue the study, perhaps using some of the books Prof. Tracy had mentioned in the class.

Lea went home with Greg over the Easter break. Helen Chambers surmised that the two were becoming more than just friends . . . she could be right!

Greg bought a copy of Robert Wright's book, *The Evolution of God.* After reading it he asked his father if he would read it so they could discuss Wright's ideas on God. His father agreed.

On Saturday, before Easter Sunday, Greg borrowed his father's car and he and Lea drove East of town on Camp Carson road. The sun was warm, the dogwood and the daffodils were in full bloom. Later they drove to Winkler's Drive-In for lunch . . . breaded tenderloin with lettuce and mayo, of course.

Life is good!

Gibson County Courthouse – Princeton, Indiana

City Library – Princeton, Indiana

First United Methodist Church – Princeton, Indiana

Princeton High School – Princeton, Indiana

Greek's Soda and Candy Store – Princeton, Indiana

Winkler's Drive-In – Princeton, Indiana

Cullom-Davis Library – Bradley University – Peoria, Illinois

Westlake Hall – Bradley University – Peoria, Illinois

Markin Recreation Center – Bradley University – Peoria, Illinois

Michel Student Center – Bradley University – Peoria, Illinois

19

Progressive Sermons

Introduction by Rev. Michael MacMillan

A Pastoral Guide for Progressive Shepherds

In his previous book, *Giving Voice to the Silent Pulpit*, my colleague Barry Blood argues convincingly that pastors trained in mainline seminaries in the past 30 years have been immersed in the latest scholarly and literary tools when it comes to the themes explored in the previous section of this book, particularly regarding beliefs in God, the Bible, prayer, miracles, Jesus as the Christ, and the Trinity, among others. However, as he also points out in *Giving Voice*, most Christian ministers have been hesitant to share this knowledge with the congregations they serve.

Based on my own pastoral experience, as well as frequent discussions with many of my fellow faith leaders, the reasons for refusing to share the latest scholarly work are not rooted in some desire to keep this new knowledge to ourselves; on the contrary, many of us would love to be able to share this fascinating information about the history and development of Christianity with a wider audience. The most common reasons for not introducing this new, groundbreaking academic work have to do with fear: Fear that the congregations we serve are just not ready to have their comfortable beliefs challenged; or, possibly, fear that the outright rejection of these new ideas by the laity will result in internal church conflict and declines in membership; or, finally and perhaps of greatest concern, fear that we will lose our jobs and livelihoods should we let a congregation know truthfully that the old theological assertions and beliefs are just not working for us personally any more.

The main reason for writing this section of the book is that we believe there are many pastors out there who would like to introduce their congregations to the latest scholarly work that they were introduced to in seminary, but who have not been able to find a workable way to do so. We're guessing there are many pastors who are seeking a new and liberating path toward intellectual and theological honesty, but who just don't know how to begin the conversation. And finally, we're guessing that there are many pastors out there who see that the traditional, old paradigm of Christianity is not only killing the individual vocational joy they have felt as faith leaders, but is actually resulting in the death of the very thing they love: the Church, as more and more people walk away from Christianity altogether.

This is a critical time for the Church, and the pastors and the leaders in congregations now have the opportunity to pave the way to a new, relevant, intellectually honest and deeply spiritual Christian experience. And while daunting, it's actually quite exciting at the same time—and well worth the effort!

After introducing you to progressive Christian thinking in the first section of this book through the teaching of Professor Tracy and his lectures and conversations with his inquiring students, our hope in this second section of the book is to offer you, as pastors and Christian leaders, some practical tools to help move your congregations into the realm of Progressive Christianity. This will not be an easy trip, but it is a necessary one, and we truly believe that you will find through this process that you are not alone in your hunger for a more meaningful and relevant Christian experience. There will be others you encounter along the way who are also there in the proverbial progressive closet with you, both within your congregations and among your clergy colleagues. So please don't ever feel as though you are alone as you consider whether or not the time is right to begin to chart a new Christian course into a brightly unfolding future.

As you begin the journey with your congregation away from the increasingly problematic traditional Christian paradigm and into the realm of Progressive Christianity, you might be asking yourself, "How and where do I begin to engage in this new conversation?" The key to answering that question is to use the wisdom and knowledge you already have of the community you currently serve to begin to discern a path forward that will engage as many folks as possible.

To be sure, this is not an overnight process! It can and should take some time and will yield the most positive results if it is a process that is not rushed. There is a sense of "pastoral patience" that you will need here to help people along this path at their own pace and willingness to go with you. Some of your congregants will follow you quickly with an eager and open mind; some will be open to some new ideas but skeptical of anything that might challenge their deeper and longer-held beliefs, and will come along more slowly; and, still others will be extremely resistant to any idea of examining their faith and Christian tradition through a progressive lens.

So how you enter into this dialog with the congregation is of the utmost importance. Take your time and pay special attention to the pulse of the congregation. The road from traditional to Progressive Christianity can be rocky, risky, and challenging, but it can also be incredibly invigorating and inspiring. In any case, it is fully necessary if we are to give the church we love a realistic hope for a meaningful future in the modern world.

The following ideas are some ways you and your congregation can begin this exciting movement into the world of Progressive Christianity. Surely there are other tools for you to use, and you will no doubt come up with your own in light of the unique congregation that you serve. But the lessons that follow have been used with success, mainly because they invite the congregation into the conversation in a non-threatening manner and encourage dialog along the way to allow people to express themselves honestly. That dialog and that expression are vitally important, for as necessary as this journey is, there is little doubt that it will be a difficult and frustrating one for many. The more often people have a chance to express what they are feeling in this process, the more meaningful and successful this transitional experience can and will be.

Theological Honesty – THE Key Ingredient

In leading your congregation from a traditional faith to a progressive spirituality, the most important single thing you can do is to be honest with the people you lead and serve. Give them a chance to enter into your own doubts and triumphs. Allow them to share your questions and concerns. What are you wrestling with when it comes to your faith? Why are you feeling called to step outside of the traditional bounds of your faith, and when did that impetus toward a more meaningful spiritual life first occur? Why do you believe this transition to be so necessary? What are some things that you learned in your seminary training that might surprise people? These are helpful questions that not only have an educational component to them, but will also let others share in your personal and religious struggles in a way that builds empathy and trust.

By honestly voicing your questions and doubts, as well as the insights and knowledge you've gained in your own personal quest, you will likely be surprised by how many of your congregants have had similar questions and are craving a new path forward in their own spiritual lives. Some may have even felt they were completely alone, but now may find that your openness and invitation to a new dialog can give them a sense of peace and hope, and the realization that they have an ally on the way. Whether you open this dialog through a sermon, a newsletter article, small group meetings, a film series or some other method, the important point is that you are honest with both your congregation and yourself about the struggles you are enduring, and how the status quo of traditional Christianity is just not working for you and many other Church members today.

The Sermon Series – A Multi-Week Primer on Progressive Christianity

One of the most helpful and meaningful ways to begin the journey into the realm of Progressive Christianity is through a multi-week sermon series that introduces elements of Christian faith as seen from a progressive viewpoint. A series like this allows you to shed light on elements of traditional Christianity that are no longer realistic in light of our current state of knowledge in the modern world. It allows you to contrast traditional versus progressive views on topics like God, sin, Jesus, prayer, salvation, heaven and hell, and many other theological topics in light of current scholarship. By the end of the sermon series, your congregation will have gained a positive appreciation of the science, historical studies, anthropology and other avenues of learning that are shaking traditional Christianity to its foundations and leading so many people to seek a different view of religion that gives new meaning to their lives.

As part of this series, pay close attention to the latest studies on religious attitudes, such as from Pew Research Studies on Religion and Life. Weave into your series often the fact those studies document of the decline of membership in Christian churches, as well as an overall decline in religious belief in general. People need to hear the urgent truth about what is happening within the church and religion in general as both face steep declines in adherents. They need to hear the stories of the "nones", those who, although they may define themselves as spiritual, claim no particular denomination or even religion as their home base because they just don't find meaning there anymore.

In light of those realities, your sermon series can then invite your congregation to re-envision the core of their faith, their love of the Jesus Way, their relationship to this awesome mystery we call "God", and a whole new way of living out their spiritual lives. A well-planned sermon series can have a lasting impact on your congregation and begin a discussion that can truly move it into the realm of Progressive Christianity.

Dialog is Central to the Process

If people are to join you on this exciting trip you are inviting them on, they will need plenty of opportunities to engage in conversation about how they are feeling and what they are grappling with, as well as what they are excited about in this new way of seeing their religious tradition. Conversations around issues of religion and theology can happen in many ways. One of the most helpful ways is through "sermon talk-back" opportunities that happen immediately following a service and offer people a fresh chance to reflect on the content of the sermon and how they felt upon experiencing it.

This accomplishes two things in particular. First, sermon talk-backs allow you, as the one offering the sermon on Progressive Christianity, a sense of freedom to challenge the traditional ways of being Christian because of the promise that people will have an immediate opportunity to respond to that challenge. It has been our experience that post-sermon reviews like this, where everyone is invited into an immediate conversation, give birth to rich and rewarding dialog. Because challenging people's long-held core religious convictions, even in the gentlest manner, with no chance for them to express themselves, can lead people to feel a sense of unease and hopelessness, the sermon talk-back will go a long way toward mitigating the distance between the sermon and whatever distress congregants might be feeling after hearing it.

The second benefit that sermon talk-backs accomplish is to demonstrate to a congregation being challenged that you have them in mind; that this is not just for you, but rather that you have deep concern for where they currently are in their own spiritual lives and how they may be struggling with what they are hearing. This shows that the challenge to move in this progressive direction is not just some whim, but rather comes from your heart and your love of the people of the church and of the church itself. Your openness, intentionality, authenticity and willingness to walk the journey together will speak volumes and keep this movement from the traditional to the progressive healthy, exciting and open.

Breaking Out of the Lectionary Prison

If you are leading a mainline, traditional Christian congregation, there is a very good chance that the people you serve have been spoon-fed a regular diet of three-year lectionary readings throughout most of their spiritual lives. They know the stories, the themes, the characters and the liturgical seasons in which they generally appear. They have likely heard these stories so many times that they have become all too familiar. Many people likely have even lost interest in them altogether because they have heard the themes repeated so many times. Even the best and freshest of preaching cannot break the monotony of the lectionary cycle for many whose entire spiritual lives have been framed within its rigid and carefully organized liturgical flow.

For many in our churches, this is likely okay. Familiarity can breed a sense of peace. But for many others who are beginning to crave a new way to envision and frame their spiritual growth, the standard lectionary cycle and the same old stories within it have ceased to inspire their imaginations. They are seeking "scripture" in a more broadened sense. They are seeking new ways to engage and channel their spiritual energy. And so it is a good thing for us that there are plenty of resources to help feed that hunger. You don't have to give up the lectionary vocabulary altogether—quitting cold turkey is never advised! But if you can begin to sprinkle in some other resources for people to draw inspiration from, we think you will be surprised by the results.

One question to ask yourself, and to discuss with your worship team if you work with one, is what other things outside of the Bible might provide a means of expressing the mystery of "God" to your congregants. What are some avenues of expression in our world through which people might have a transcendent experience of that which seems awe-inspiring to the point of being what we so often call "Holy"? The Biblical scriptures tell stories of people throughout time who have had experiences of this nature in their lives: Moses, Joseph,

Jacob, Sarah, Jesus, Mary and Paul just to name a few. And our spiritual experience as Christians has been framed by the stories told about them and their ideas of who this mystery is that we name "God".

But what other stories are we missing out on that might spark a deeply spiritual moment for those who attend our churches? What might it mean, for example, to begin introducing poems as scripture? Or visual arts, such as paintings and sculptures? How about photographs of the natural world, or of people coming together in times of need? From the world of the visual arts in its great variety, to poetry and short stories, to film clips and photography, to non-canonical scriptures and the texts of other religious traditions that we share this world with, there is a trove of resources in which the mystery of "God" and a deeply meaningful spiritual essence can be experienced. Progressive Christianity is open to the idea of alternative scriptures, and so are many of those who attend our churches.

Theological Grime and the Importance of Language

As you begin to invite your congregation on the journey from traditional to Progressive Christianity, the issue of language is going to become a major factor in determining the degree to which people resonate with the spiritual places you are leading them into and how readily they are able go along with you. There is a kind of balancing act that will have to be maintained as you and your congregation begin the process of envisioning something new, while still being framed within the more traditional paradigm of the Christian way as you have been living up to this point.

If you are like a majority of mainline congregations, that experience is likely to revolve around a Sunday morning worship service of some kind, with all the usual liturgical elements and language. Obviously you will not change this overnight, nor should you feel the need to. You and your congregation will figure this out as you undertake the journey over time. But, the language that you use during the transition from traditional to progressive will be vitally important.

The recently departed progressive theologian Marcus Borg, in his book *Speaking Christian: Why Christian Words Have Lost Their Meaning and Power – and How They Can Be Restored,* argued:

> *How we speak and understand Christian language matters. It can change and revitalize our understanding of what Christianity is about. It also matters for those Christians for whom its conventional meanings have become so problematic that some have stopped using biblical and Christian language...if we avoid the language of our faith because of uncertainty about what it means, we grant a monopoly on it to those who are most certain about its meaning. That would be unfortunate, for the language is extraordinarily rich, wide and transformative. (pg. 234).*

What Borg is saying, in other words, is that a great deal of our theological language is coated with theological "grime" from historical contexts that don't speak meaningfully to us any more. This means that our words and concepts, while still important, may have to be sanded down of that grime from long ago, taken back to their bare essence, and then reapplied to our times and contexts today to seek a sense of modern meaning. Some words, you may find, will not fit where you and your congregation are any more. Some language, on the other hand, may become even more powerful as you and your congregation better understand its history and its reasons for being a part of the Christian tradition. Either way, you won't know the full import of these words in modern life until you go there and begin to explore the language of our faith and then reapply it to your community again today.

Part of this exploration will involve asking what particular words mean that we have likely used without a thought in the past. For instance, what does it mean to call what we do "worship"? What, or whom, are we worshipping? What does worship mean in a progressive theological model? Is what we do when we gather as congregations worship? Or is it something else, and if so, what then do we call it? Worship has a particular connotation, especially in terms of keeping alive and well the traditional vision of a supernatural god that needs or demands some kind of an appeasement. How about even the name/title "God"? What does this mean in today's religiously diverse world?

One way to begin to explore what "God" is, is to ask your congregants to envision two ways of experiencing their spiritual life in terms of what we call "God". Ask them to explore one idea of God in terms of *belief*, and how it feels for the heart of their spiritual lives to be all about belief in God as a distant, heavenly judge and protector, as we have been trained to do within our tradition. And then contrast that idea with *experience*, making the core of the spiritual life about actually encountering this mystery we call "God" rather than belief. How does it feel for them to put aside the need to believe, and enter into the realm of presence and sensation when it comes to their relationship with that which we name "God?" These are two very different spiritual ways of living.

How about the concept of Sin? What does that idea mean to progressive Christians committed to a belief in the basic goodness and dignity of mankind? How about Prayer? What is prayer when there is no supernatural god in the sky to pray to? How about Salvation? What are we being saved from if there is no fiery Hell with an eternal afterlife of horrific suffering? We could go on and on, but you probably get the point.

How you frame these words and concepts that have been handed down to you from traditional Christianity, and in which you and your congregation have been immersed, is of the utmost importance in determining how you will pave your roadway towards Progressive Christianity. A fresh, new and invigorating spiritually progressive path cannot be paved with the stones of the traditional faith. First those stones have to be unearthed, examined, sanded down of their historical grime, and then polished and reset in a way that grounds people in the experience of being Christian in the modern world, without the stumbling blocks of the past. Language is of critical importance in how we traverse this pathway to a progressive future.

Words for the Journey

In the following pages we have included a sampling of sermons from one church that is in the process of shifting from the traditional to the progressive in terms of how they live out their spiritual lives as Christians. These sample sermons come from an eight-week sermon series they entered into titled "What is Progressive Christianity?" The series was intentionally constructed to help the congregation understand both the limitations and challenges of traditional Christianity in our times, along with the excitement of a new way of seeing and experiencing the Christianity that they knew and loved, yet felt disconnected from.

The worship services, or Weekly Gatherings as they were called, were intentionally designed to reflect a more progressive viewpoint. Language and words were carefully crafted to avoid the taint of theism. Experience in these times of gathering took preference over belief and recitation of formulaic creeds. And most importantly, dialogs taking the form of immediate sermon talk-backs were held each week to allow for the congregants to express their concerns, their confusion, their frustrations, their moments of enlightenment and their joy at this way of entering anew into their Christian faith.

It was an exciting time for this church, as it helped crystallize and make more concrete the journey that it had been on in small ways for the past decade. That evolution is still ongoing, and there are still hurdles and struggles for sure, but because of the authenticity, honesty and intentionality given to the process of this transition from the traditional to the progressive, the church is growing, thriving and expanding in wonderful ways.

As you set out to follow in their brave and inquiring footsteps, please feel free to use as much or as little of the following sermon material as you find helpful in your quest to move your congregation from the struggling, traditional paradigm to a more vibrant, progressive view. These sermons are intended as examples to give you ideas and starter topics. You may agree with some of these suggestions and question others, so please keep in mind they are here simply to stimulate your thinking as you tailor the sermons to the needs and receptivity of your own church and congregants.

As you and your church make this life-changing and essential transformation from traditional to Progressive Christianity, we wish you peace and courage as together we set the course for a liberated and thriving future for this faithful and spiritual way of being that we love.

—)(—

Sermon #1 - What is Progressive Christianity?

Scripture - *Mark 12: 13-17; Matthew 25: 35-40; Luke 6: 27-30 & John 8: 1-11*

In the opening chapter of his book "Progressive Faith and Practice," author and pastor Roger Ray tells the story of a philosophy professor who came into his freshman classroom on the first day of class and announced, "This room is filled with four foot tall Skrinchen." "They are", the professor went on, "without mass and invisible to you, and visible only to me." Commenting on this memory, Roger Ray goes on to explain how the professor was trying to make a point to his freshman class about what we call an *a priori* truth claim, or a claim that needs no evidence to be verified, and which cannot be subjected to any sort of test to verify the claims of its legitimacy. The claim is just to be believed and accepted based on what someone has told you.

Roger Ray goes on to say that "though there was no way to prove that the room was *not* full of Skrinchen, there was also no particular reason to believe he was telling the truth." He goes on to say, "I knew that I would be foolish to believe that I was surrounded by these invisible beings. It would take me another decade to have the courage to apply this same conclusion to what I had been told by my Sunday School teachers about angels, demons, a talking snake and so much more."[19]

You could add a lot more to that list—virgin births, parted waters, bringing people back to life, turning water into wine—but I think you get the point. Roger Ray's Skrinchen story is a great way to begin our journey into what we call "Progressive Christianity", because the allure of just believing in things, whether they be Skrinchens or other myths and stories that have come down to us in our religion, and suspending our rational faculties (history, science, biblical criticism, literature studies) is exactly what Progressive Christianity is trying to raise awareness against.

In the coming several weeks, under the umbrella of Progressive Christianity, we will explore several big theological topics. We will begin with God, and ask: "What is this thing, this *mystery* we call God, and how is that he/she/it (pick your favorite) became related to us and our world or universe?" Is God to be believed in like Skrinchens, or is God an experience available to us all through practice?

We will then explore this prophet and radical named Jesus of Nazareth, the one we commonly refer to as the *Christ*, or the anointed one. How did this Galilean Jewish peasant come to be the Christ, the Messiah, God's son, the one eternally begotten by God the Father, the Lamb of God who takes away the sins of the world, and even finally, the ultimate judge of a fallen creation? I have a feeling Jesus would be a little surprised if he came back today to hear how exalted he was! How does it change things if we see Jesus as a person who experienced the Divine so deeply that he called us to walk a similar path, rather than just believing proclaimed "truths" about him?

Following our exploration of Jesus, we will journey into the Bible, this book that many of us have been raised to believe is the ultimate marker for our relationship with God or, as I have been told,

---

[19] Ray, Roger, *Progressive Faith and Practice*, 1-2.

the *only* book you will ever need! How can we find meaning in this book while recognizing it for the limited, contextual, historical and very human product that it is? Following our honest exploration of the Bible, we will then spend a week on the S-word (two S-words, actually) that are tied together and forever held over our heads by our religious tradition: Sin and Salvation. How might our vision of the world and our way in it change if we did not see ourselves as fallen and in need of redemption?

Finally, we will examine prayer, asking what are we doing when we pray and, more specifically, what prayer means to a Progressive Christian. In our modern world, does it still make sense to appease or appeal to a Supreme Being in the clouds who doles out rewards and punishments? And if not, how might the idea of prayer still be meaningful in our lives and relationships?

Along the way we will touch on many topics: faith, evil, the Trinity, the cross, worship, justice and more. And in the end, I am hoping we can lay the foundation for our future as a progressive church and begin to chart a new course to be real leaders and proponents of Progressive Christianity. For I am convinced that without it, without what Progressive Christianity brings to the table, the whole thing—the church and its earliest message of love and inclusion—is going to continue to disappear into the night.

And why would I say that? I am not trying to exaggerate these concerns simply to instill fear—God knows we have enough of that in our lives through our current doomsday politics and religion! But we do need to be real about the state of the church, simply for the necessity of moving forward. Depending on what research you look at, sources say that anywhere from 75 to 90 percent of churches in the US are in a state of stagnation, meaning no growth, or are actually declining in membership year after year. There are statistics showing that between 4,000 and 7,000 churches close their doors each year, compared to only 1,000 to 2,000 new church starts per year. Some surveys have found that of adults who responded, only 30 percent or so said they attend a church regularly, though many believe the number is closer to 20 percent, or one in five.[20]

There are a number of possible explanations as to why this trend is continuing and getting worse by the year. One answer is that there are too many other competing demands on people's time. Another likely factor is that continuing stories of clergy abuse have shaken people's faith in their churches and church leaders. Still another reason is self-directed spirituality, meaning people exploring on their own a variety of options and resources for their spiritual journey that does not involve a church and a choir or anything traditional.

These are all compelling arguments, and all are likely true to a point. But one major reason I believe that people, especially younger generations, are not flocking to church communities is because the things that churches are teaching adults and kids about God are just not corresponding with what the realms of science and history are teaching people about life, the human condition, the universe and the cosmos in relation to the mystery of God. This idea that the Bible is the Word of God, or that Jesus died for our sins, or that he was born of a virgin, or that the only path to God is through faith in Jesus Christ, or ideas of judgment and good and bad places where one goes—all of these ancient claims of our current, ancient religious paradigm are simply not relevant any more to your average, modern mind.

The number of church closings and the accelerating rate of declining membership within active churches means that people are done with the fear that stems from these myths. And it's happening to all churches. We always hear how the mega-churches are growing like crazy, but that is not true anymore. The fact is that whether we are talking about mega-churches, or liberal mainline protestant churches, Catholic churches, Baptist churches, or even Evangelical churches, they are all in decline and fast becoming relics of the past. And I am

---

[20] Online sources, Churchleadership.org: *http://www.churchleadership.org/ apps/ articles/ default.asp? articleid=42346/*, Pew Forum *http://www.pewforum.org/ 2015/05/12/americas-changing-religious-landscape/*, CNN.com: *http://www.cnn.com/2015/05/12/living/pew-religion-study/index.html*

convinced that the main reason, as Roger Ray pointed out, is because Skrinchens just don't make sense anymore. People are sick and tired of being told what to believe, and being told that belief in doctrines from long ago is what the crux of your relationship to God is about. They are seeking a deeper connection, something fresher and more meaningful. They are seeking mystery, experience and inter-connection to the world around them in their spiritual lives. And that is exactly what Progressive Christianity can offer.

What I want to accomplish today, in light of the decline of churches of the more traditional theological outlook, is to get a grasp of just what Progressive Christianity is and why it is different than traditional Christianity. To do that, I want to paraphrase a video from a man named Fred Plumer, a former United Church of Christ Minister and President of the organization *ProgressiveChristianity.org*. In this seven-minute video, available online,[21] Fred begins to dispel the myth that Progressive Christianity is something brand new. Progressive Christianity, rather, has a history that goes back over one hundred years, to a time when clergy, theologians and seminary professors in the late 19th and early 20th centuries actively called themselves progressive.

These Christians, Plumer says, were passionate about re-thinking Christianity in light of the new, natural scientific evidence of the times, and they continued to promote the rise of modern biblical scholarship that had begun during the 1800's. One thinker in particular, Rev. Henry Emerson Fosdick, thought that if our understanding of Christianity did not align itself with the scientific breakthroughs and Biblical scholarship that had been done, it would die and go away. Where we find ourselves today, Plumer points out, is in a similar place. Therefore, he says that for his organization *(progressivechristianity.org)*, Progressive Christianity requires a willingness to take a look at the best scholarship, whether it's in the fields of science, theology, history and others, and to examine our current beliefs and, if need be, to change our thinking about what Christianity is today.

---

[21] Plumer, *Progressivechristianity.org*

Plumer talks about how Progressive Christianity can be a bit hard to define, and how it is not uncommon for some Christians to label themselves as "progressive", even though they are not actually progressive *Christians*. In reality they may be politically or socially progressive, but they are not theologically progressive. And their religious outlook remains much as it has been throughout their lives. Their Christology and their theology (*theology focusing on God and Christology focusing on Jesus as the Christ*) have not changed very much. This creates a challenge in defining Progressive Christianity.

Plumer argues that if we are willing to examine the best scholarship with a rational and open mind, whether it be biblical, theological, historical or scientific, and somehow be willing to make a change or adjust our thinking about what Christianity really means, this fits the category of "progressive" in the theological sense. That is why for Plumer's organization, the focus is on theology and Christology. They see these as the two central issues that need to be re-thought for the church to continue to have meaning. To fail to do so is for the church to become irrelevant.

By focusing on these two issues and examining them through the best scholarship, they hope to reconstruct a new type of Christianity that fits not only what we understand about who Jesus *was*, but also what Jesus *is* in the context of the 21st century. Plumer says that Jesus gave us a path, and that Jesus was teaching us that if we practice that path in our lives, we will open ourselves to some of the same experiences of the divine that Jesus had. By following that path, our relationships with other people, with creation, and with the environment all change. It is in the end about trying to dissolve boundaries between us, to shed our dualistic mentality where we see the "other" as something different than ourselves, and begin to see instead divine, sacred, God-ness in all things. This means a great change in our attitudes from where we currently stand as Christians.

Finally, Plumer dispels the myth that Progressive Christians are basically atheistic. This is not true. He talks about his belief that there is a spirit, that there is something that is greater than we can possibly explain or understand, and that it is our attempt to actually experience that mystery that Jesus was guiding us towards. In the end, Progressive Christianity is not about belief. It is about traveling along a path in community with fresh eyes to see another reality that can truly change the world.

In listening to Plumer, it's easy to come to see the term 'Progressive Christianity' as redundant. Because wasn't Christianity progressive in its earliest days? I mean the word "progressive", and its root *progress*, when you set aside the modern political connotations, simply means to move forward, to seek to change things for the better, to improve on things. To progress means there is a desire to change, to reform, rather than to seek to keep things the way they are. If you bring those ideas together with Christianity, then you arrive at this definition from Wikipedia.

> *Progressive Christianity is a form of Christianity which is characterized by a willingness to question tradition, an acceptance of human diversity, a strong emphasis on social justice and care for the poor and the oppressed, and environmental stewardship of the Earth.*[22]

Even though this is a modern definition, it sounds a lot like Christianity from its earliest days. This was a church very different from the ways of the world in the first century: inclusive, striving for communal equality, sharing things in common, proclaiming a crucified Jewish man more powerful than the Kings and Caesars of the day. All of this shows that Christianity was a progressive movement from its beginning.

And the early Church was modeled on the life and teachings of Jesus, who lived and breathed a progressive lifestyle. Listen to what a couple of Westar Institute Scholars wrote:

---

[22] Wikipedia

The historical Jesus was a progressive teacher who raised important questions and sought fresh answers. Using rhetorical strategies such as parables and aphorisms that employ humor to undercut and undermine the powerful political structures of his day, Jesus envisioned an alternative way to look at the world, a so-called Domain of God.[23]

So when we hear stories of Jesus' inclusive meals, or his breaking barriers among relations with women, or touching the sick and the untouchable, or speaking out against greed and poverty, he was ushering in a progressive way to see the world that was very different from the context of his day. We always need to keep that in mind, especially during this series. Before there were creeds to believe; before there were formulas to assent to; before there were litmus tests of belief; before Jesus became the New Adam, or was transformed into the Lamb of God; before all of that there was just this progressive Jesus and later this progressive church turning the world upside down with a vision of love, peace, hope, inclusion and justice. Christianity has been progressive since its earliest days, and it's about time we reclaim that fact.

For the sake of the church, both our church and the Church overall, I hope we can let go of the Skrinchens of ancient religious dogmas and all of the theological verbal grime that comes with them, and get back on the progressive Jesus path that he called us to in the first place. Because if we can, that Realm of God that Jesus so often spoke of will bloom right before our eyes and this world will change for the better. And we can be leaders in paving the way to that joyful realm. I hope you enjoy this sermon series. And please stick around following our service each week to dialog, talk about your feelings and reactions, express what you are challenged by and excited by, and keep the conversation going. Amen

---

[23] Jones, Paul/Kea, Perry, *A Progressive Jesus*

Sermon #2 - What is This Thing Called God? - Part One

Proverbs – *Proverbs 9: 10*

Welcome to the second sermon of our series that is exploring the question: "What is Progressive Christianity?" I hope you will enjoy and be challenged by this series and perhaps find a new way of conceiving our lives in relation to this mystery we generally call "God". Last week we accomplished a few things. First, we honestly confronted the fact that the Church in every facet is dying. This is just a fact. Second, we defined Progressive Christianity as a theological movement, not a political movement, and laid out a working definition of it as a spiritual way of being that examines religious claims through the rational faculties of science, history, linguistic studies, globalization, technology and other areas of study and knowledge.

We defined Progressive Christianity as "a form of Christianity which is characterized by a willingness to question tradition, an acceptance of human diversity, a strong emphasis on social justice and care for the poor and the oppressed, and environmental stewardship of the Earth."[24] And finally, we examined how both Jesus and the earliest Christian communities, based on that definition, were actually "progressive" from their very earliest days. Our tradition, as it has been handed down to us, has just lost sight of that fact for a variety of reasons, both intentional and unintentional.

Today, in the first of two parts on God, we will get a little more specific, and examine the question: Just what is this thing we call God? What do we mean when we say God, specifically for us as Christians? In 2014, the results from a Pew Research Poll Study showed that 89 percent of Americans "believe in God or a Universal Spirit."[25] These numbers are down from 92 percent in 2007, but that is still a lot of people who *believe* in God!

---

[24] Wikipedia

[25] Pewforum.org

My question is: What God do they believe in? To me there's a big difference in how Pew phrased the question, as they said "God *or* a Universal Spirit". In my thinking, these are entirely different concepts in most people's minds. Today then, is about exploring the first of these, the God I think most believe in, the God of what we might call Supernatural Theism. Marcus Borg tells us "Supernatural theism imagines God as a person-like being, an exceedingly superlative person-like being, indeed *the* supreme being." He goes on to say "A long time ago, this person-like being created the world as something separate from God. Thus God and the world are sharply distinguished: God is 'up in heaven,' out there, beyond the universe."[26] That's a good definition of Supernatural Theism, and again the God most people interviewed in the Pew Poll likely believe in.

And yet, that view is highly problematic, as I hope to show in just a bit. This Supernatural God is the focus of this week. Next week, we will focus on the God I think the Pew Research Center meant with the phrase Universal Spirit. Universal Spirit is a good term for God as conceived of within the Progressive Christian movement. It sees God very differently, not as the Father in the Sky, but rather as the Ground of Being, or the Creative Impulse of the Universe, or even of the Universe Becoming Alive. This is what we call a Panentheistic view of God, one that sees God not just "out there", as Supernatural Theism does, but that sees God as both worldly and transcendent all at the same time, exhausted by neither, present in both.

This is what the great theologian Paul Tillich meant when he shocked the theological world by declaring that "God does not exist". He wrote this: "God does not exist. God is rather being itself beyond essence and existence."[27] He was quickly labeled an atheist by those who could not quite grasp what he was saying, which was that if God exists, then God is finite, because existence is finite.

---

[26] Borg, Marcus, *The Heart of Christianity*, 65

[27] Tillich, Paul, *Systematic Theology*, 205.

By questioning the existence of a supernatural God, Tillich points us toward the possibility of an even more powerful, infinite presence in the universe and in our lives, one not limited by a body, or emotions, or by a human form that may someday cease to exist as all finite things do. By unshackling our concept of God from its human limitations, he changed theology forever, whether people liked it or not. He declared the supernatural theistic God dead and allowed people to envision something much more meaningful. This is the vision of God we will focus on next week.

Before going on, I have a confession to make. One of my favorite things to do in a theological conversation is to tell people that I, an ordained minister, do not "believe" in God. It's true—I don't. This leaves people pretty surprised, and I love the perplexed expressions! "What do you mean you don't believe in God?" they always say. I explain to them that what I mean is that I do not believe in a God of supernatural theism, the God that is often interpreted from the all-too-human stories of the Bible. I tell them that for me, believing in this God just does nothing for me, that I am much more intrigued by the *experience* of the divine through love, awe, mystery, and interconnection; that I find "God" in the extraordinary, or the miraculous nature of the ordinary, or in acts of justice and relationship. That is where the divine spark glows brightest for me, and where I experience this mystery we call "God" most powerfully.

Inevitably, this conversation comes around to the Bible, and they say, surely as a Pastor I believe in the God of the Bible, right? And then I usually shock them again as I tell them "It is precisely *because* of the Bible that I don't believe in this kind of God". Often the conversation ends right there! Now I often don't get the chance to explain myself in these conversations, but I have the chance here, and therefore want to flesh out what I mean by those statements, and in doing so build a case against the God of supernatural theism, the God of the Bible. I want to do this through two main ideas, because they are both central to how so many believe in God today. And they are both extremely damaging when they are carried to their logical conclusions.

First, a group of us undertook a journey last year that we called "The Bible in a Year Study", where we read through the entirety of the Bible from beginning to end. We then got together once a month to talk about what we had discovered. It was a fascinating journey, and in the end I think a handful of us actually completed the reading/study with detailed notes! When we met to discuss what we had read, the conversations were always fascinating in scope and depth. One theme in particular kept resonating among the group, especially by those who diligently read and took notes. That theme was God, and especially the seemingly endless jealousy, pettiness and obscene violence that this Biblical God wreaked on the world in both the Hebrew Scriptures and in the Newer Testament. And I think this surprised people, as evidenced by how often this theme was brought up by the group. I mean, sure, we were all taught as kids the cute little story of this God of the Bible telling Noah to build an ark, collect a bunch of animals and how then God sent the rains and drowned all of the inhabitants of earth that were not on that ark. Nothing says "cute little Sunday school story for kids" like an angry father mass drowning his family. Yet I grew up, like many of you, coloring pictures of this!

And we all know of Sodom and Gomorrah, where God firebombs a town for their decadent ways, even turning poor Lot's wife into a pillar of salt for having the gall to look back. These are familiar to most, if not all, Christians. We learned these stories as kids, as twisted as that may seem, and carried these morbid biblical tales into adulthood, without modification, as the foundation of our spiritual lives.

But those who read further than Genesis and these particular well-known issues of violence learned a lot more about our God of the Bible and His apparent thirst for violence that makes Attila the Hun look like a peace worker. What follows is just a tiny sampling. First, for instance, there is the familiar story of God killing all of the firstborn children in Egypt (Exodus 12:29), one of many awful things God inflicted upon the Egyptians. God then goes on to drown the Egyptian army in the parted waters of the Red Sea. Thousands and thousands killed (Exodus 14: 23-28). Or how about this story from Exodus (32:

25-29), a not-so-wonderful depiction of our loving Biblical God:

When Moses saw that the people were running wild (for Aaron had let them run wild, to the derision of their enemies), then Moses stood in the gate of the camp, and said, "Who is on the Lord's side? Come to me!" And all the sons of Levi gathered around him. He said to them, "Thus says the Lord, the God of Israel, 'Put your sword on your side, each of you! Go back and forth from gate to gate throughout the camp, and each of you kill your brother, your friend, and your neighbor.'" The sons of Levi did as Moses commanded, and about three thousand of the people fell on that day. Moses said, "Today you have ordained yourselves for the service of the Lord, each one at the cost of a son or a brother, and so have brought a blessing on yourselves this day".*

Or how about in the Book of Numbers (16:49), as the people of God have the audacity to whine and complain that God keeps killing them, and how this is just not fair. A quick read will show you that God ends that conversation by sending a plague, and killing 14,000 more of them to stop their complaining!

And then in Second Chronicles (13:13-17), we find the story of the great King of Judah, Abijah, who was at war with the Northern Kingdom of Israel *(Remember there were two kingdoms in this time: Judah and Israel)*. In this story, we are told how God favors the King of Judah, and helps his army slaughter the Israelites in a great battle. In the end, when the dust settles, we are told that 500,000 people died because of God's intervention. That's a lot of people killed by this intervening, supernatural God!

Let's do one more, though we could literally do this all day! My personal favorite "God killing people" story from the Bible comes from Joshua (10: 8-11). I'll read it to you so you know I am not making this all up:

So Joshua went up from Gilgal, he and all the fighting force with him, all the mighty warriors. The Lord said to Joshua, "Do not fear them, for I have handed them over to you; not one of them shall stand before you." So Joshua came upon them suddenly, having marched up all night from Gilgal. And the Lord threw them into a panic before Israel, who inflicted a great slaughter on them at Gibeon, chased them by the way of the ascent of Beth-horon, and struck them down as far as Azekah and Makkedah. As they fled before Israel, while they were going down the slope of Beth-horon, the Lord threw down huge stones from heaven on them as far as Azekah, and they died; there were more who died because of the hailstones than the Israelites killed with the sword.

In this story, God not only sets the violence and carnage in motion, but actually participates in the killing, in fact slaughtering more people than the army did by throwing down huge stones from heaven! This story adds new meaning to the line "let he who is without sin cast the first stone".

All told, when you add up all of the deaths at the hand of God in the Bible, our Holy Book, the Word of God as many tell you, you get around twenty, maybe twenty five *million* or so people massacred. A little side note for you: the Devil, or Satan, or the Adversary, as he is known in his many forms—do you know how many deaths he was responsible for? Ten. Job's seven sons and three daughters, and surely those could be laid at this Biblical God's feet as well. From the Noah story, to the sending of Jesus into the world to die for our sins, to other stories like the killing of Ananias and Sapphira for withholding property in the Book of Acts, I think we have made a pretty clear case that the God of the Bible has a bit of a violence problem.

And I, for one, cannot base my spiritual life on a bloodthirsty deity like this. I know this might be difficult for many of you to absorb, but we must do so honestly, for only in an honest engagement of our sacred stories, will we find the courage to move in a new direction in terms of our faith and begin to see God anew.[28]

My second big problem with the God of supernatural theism comes from quotes I have seen on memes and on people's Facebook and Twitter posts or even billboards along the highways. These are generally widely held beliefs from Christians about God. One phrase I remember seeing somewhere goes like this:

God has a reason for allowing things to happen. We may never understand His wisdom, but we simply have to trust His will.

Given the amount of violence and pain and grief in this world, the idea that this supernatural deity *could* intervene, but chooses not to, and not only that, but that some of this is *His* will, and the reason will later become clear to us, well that is just sick, twisted logic, my friends. But you hear it all the time.

Another expression of faith I hear from time to time, and one that is a huge problem for the model of a supernatural theistic God, is summed up in this phrase: *"Sometimes God doesn't change your situation, because He's trying to change your heart."* In other words, God could intervene to save your child, or to cure you or a loved one of cancer, or to stop a genocidal maniac, or to give you food when you're starving, or to remedy countless other crises, but God deliberately chooses not to do so in order to teach you a lesson about life.

Are we to believe that God leaves some in this world in poverty or slavery or oppression for the purpose of *changing their hearts?* Again, God *could* change your situation, but has made a choice to allow you to suffer because the brutality will be a good learning experience for you. That's even more twisted than the previous idea that God's will allows awful things to happen to good people for 'his' own secret reasons! Whoever thinks that human suffering is God's intent may be desperately seeking an explanation for traumatic events in their own lives, but that idea in relation to God must be carried beyond them to the rest of the

---

[28] New Revised Standard Version translation, 1989

world as well. And think then, of some of those times this God did *not* intervene: the Holocaust, 9-11, Rwandan Genocide, Hurricane Katrina, etc. The list could go on and on.

The God of supernatural theism that so many believe they have no alternative to, as we have just seen, is a tribal, bloodthirsty deity that chooses to intervene in some people's or countries' or cultures' pain, but refuses to in others. And I cannot ever believe in, or base my spiritual life on, a deity like this.

I rest my case now against this God, and all the proof you need is right there in the Bible. This is the tough stuff, friends. This can be really challenging and can shake us to the core of our spirituality. You may even feel like Humpty Dumpty falling off the wall, wondering if your faith can all be put together again after an honest encounter with the God of the Bible. But through this kind of honest reflection on the traditional teachings of our theistic religion, we come to the realization that this is not all there is to our spiritual life *just* because it says so in the Bible, or just because our religious paradigm tells us so. There is so much more to this awesome mystery we name God, and this honest encounter can be the stuff of liberation and the invitation to walk a new spiritual path, or even a re-birth of your spiritual identity.

And keep in mind, being put back together again is not necessarily the goal. Being transformed, rather, and beginning to see yourself as one with this mystery we name God in a new way you were never encouraged to do before—*that* is the goal. It's time we stop living with the mentality of our reading from Proverbs: "The Fear of the Lord is the Beginning of Wisdom". Fear has no place here, and it's not of God. We fear an abusive parent; we fear someone who promises or commits violence; we fear those who threaten us; and we especially fear those who we believe have this supreme power to mess up our lives or even to end them, if they so choose, to teach us a lesson. Fear of the Lord is *not* the beginning of wisdom, but the end result of an idolatry that religions for millennia have allowed to masquerade as God. Well, that time of fear is over, and the time has come for fear to be conquered by a progressive Christian vision that speaks a strong message of love and life and oneness instead.

I want to close with a paragraph from progressive theologian Roger Ray, who wrote this on the need to jettison worn-out and tired beliefs in a supernatural God. He wrote:

> *In the hope of preserving credible, meaningful and relevant faith in the twenty-first century, let's stop trying to limit God to our own religion, stop trying to manipulate the Divine into doing our bidding, punishing our enemies or rewarding our friends. Let's take our foot off of God's throat, because, you know, God doesn't have a throat, and we look pretty silly trying to hold the Spirit down.*[29]

Amen.

Sermon #3 - What is This Thing Called God? - Part Two
Scripture - *Acts 17: 6-28*

In the previous part of our series on Progressive Christianity, we began to explore the idea of God, asking in particular "What is this thing called God?" When I started working on that sermon, I quickly realized that unless we wanted to be here for a very long time, that was going to have be a two-part sermon. Even two parts falls woefully short of a complete exploration of this mystery we name God in light of the tools of Progressive Christianity: historical research, scientific inquiry, linguistic study, literature analysis, biblical criticism, sociology, archaeology and other areas of study that must be brought to any exploration of such an audacious question. So, in Part I of "What Is God?", we began to examine this question by focusing really on "what God is *not*." For we must first understand the problems and limitations of our traditional

---

[29] Ray, Roger, *Progressive Faith*, Eugene, 17

"God" framework before we can begin to envision something quite different and break out of that paradigm.

We looked at the God of what we called supernatural theism, or the God that has come to us from the Bible, the one so many believe in literally, and the one that an increasing number of people refuse to believe in at all. We explored this God in light of the stories of violence throughout the Bible, beginning with the awful story of drowning the Earth's inhabitants in Genesis, to stories in which God literally throws down stones from the heavens onto the enemies of Israel, to countless other stories in which God inflicts violence upon humanity for a whole variety of reasons.

I concluded that this God of supernatural theism is not only irrelevant to the modern mind, but even more importantly this God is dangerous, as proven through a lust for tribalism and violence and nationalism that knows no end. We also examined views held by many people of this God of the Bible, such as the idea that God doesn't give us more than we can handle; or that God puts obstacles in our way like cancer, illness, debt, difficult people, the death of loved one and more life tragedies, for the purpose of teaching us some lesson, or to make us stronger.

I described this as a sick and twisted notion, and one that when applied universally, as it must be, draws the picture of a God who chooses to intervene in some people's lives, saving, healing and helping some, but refusing to do so in the lives of others. This is the Tribal God of supernatural theism that we explored last week. And based on the amount of feedback and excitement so many of you offered during our post-sermon dialog, it became clear that many of you felt the freedom, perhaps for the first time, to acknowledge that you have had problems with this "God" and that it's time for the Tribal God, the literal God of the Bible, to be retired.

Now I want to make a further clarification, and we will get more into this when we examine the Bible. The tribal, supernatural God that I am talking about here is not just one homogenous conception that is the same from the book of Genesis right through to Revelation. Keep in mind that when we are speaking of the God of the Bible, we are really describing a conglomerate of images and interpretations of a supreme being by human beings throughout the course of several millennia, as ideas of this God were borrowed, adapted, created, re-created, tweaked, and interpreted.

Therefore there is no *one* God presented in the Bible. That is just not honest to the development of the scriptures. In the Hebrew Scriptures alone, we have a minimum of four distinct sources all woven together, each conveying a drastically different portrayal of God, much as the Newer Testament's four Gospels paint very different pictures of who Jesus was. This is why there are two different creation stories, and two ark stories, and all sorts of contradictions and omissions from one story to the next.

This deity then, which we call God, is a composite of human longings, hopes, fears, hatreds, historical circumstances, fantasies, and cultural biases by which we describe our limited understanding of the universe. So when I talk of retiring the God of the Bible, which might seem a bit of a threatening endeavor to some of you, what I really mean is that we need to retire the ancient limitations and constrictions and anthropomorphisms, meaning the attribution of all-too-human characteristics to a personal god or deity, based on one particular culture or another. We are still doing this today. How often is God equated with freedom and America, for instance? Quite often. We also need to keep in mind that the name "God" is not a proper name, but a symbol or metaphor that should point beyond itself to some kind of ultimate reality that transcends our tribe, our cultures, our borders, or our nations.

To keep this god named "God" of the Bible around just keeps tribalism and global division alive and well in an age that is becoming more and more globalized and diverse. We've come too far for that as a world. Joseph Campbell summed it up well, when he said, "God is an ambiguous word in our language because it appears to refer to something that is known. But the transcendent is unknown, and unknowable. God is transcendent, finally, of anything like the name

'God'. God is beyond names and forms."[30]

He goes on to quote the great mystic Meister Eckhart, who said that "the ultimate and highest leave-taking is, leaving 'God' for God, leaving your notion of God for an experience of that which transcends all notions."[31]

Sounds a bit like what Carl Jung meant, when he said "religion is a defense against the experience of God."[32] Our religious beliefs, handed down to us as though they contain all of the truth we will ever need, imprison us and hold us hostage, holding us back from pondering the essence of something so much more awe-inspiring in terms of God, or even punishing us or branding us if we dare to do so.

And as I look around, I think often we are okay with that, because it's just so much easier to believe in something concrete, and to think we have all the answers, than it is to grapple with the experience of the intimate and un-knowable nature of this mystery that we name "God". We like our answers and structures and systems tidied up in a neat little box. And in the end, when it comes to the God of the Bible and Christian theology, that gives us supernatural theism, and a bearded father in the sky that, oddly enough, seems an awful lot like us.

I came across another Pew Research Poll that was conducted very recently.[33] It focused on the category of people they call "Nones." Nones are a rapidly growing group of people who are religiously unaffiliated, and now either identify as atheists, agnostics, or just as people who don't find meaning in organized religion any more. They now make up an estimated 23 percent of the population according to Pew, and that number is rapidly growing. An even more relevant finding for us in our examination of Progressive Christianity is the fact that, of

---

[30] Campbell, Joseph, *The Power of Myth*, 56

[31] Ibid, 56-57

[32] Ibid, 261

[33] *www.pewresearch.org*

all of the Nones that Pew polled, an astounding half of them had been raised in a traditional religious manner, with a church, synagogue, mosque or temple centering their religious life.

Although they have many reasons for abandoning their former faiths, the Poll found that 36 percent of these previously religious Nones had *not* left those institutions because they were busy with lives or sports (the things churches like us tell ourselves to make ourselves feel good!). Rather, they left because all of this religious, personal God stuff is just too unbelievable. They left because they see that science and other branches of modern knowledge have shown that all of this personal God in the sky stuff, and ideas of heaven and hell, sin and salvation, and judgment and condemnation, just don't make sense in today's world and are not remotely relevant for their lives. The Nones, as I mentioned, are *the* fastest growing religious category. This doesn't bode well for the future of Supernatural Theism and the idea of a personal God. I think it might be time for a new vision.

Speaking of this idea of a personal God, I came across an illuminating exchange in *The Power of Myth* interview series, between Joseph Campbell and Bill Moyers as they are having a conversation about this tribal deity we name God and our need to make God personal—meaning to relate to God as a person, with all of the very human attributes that come along with that idea. This in turn always leads one on the path of supernatural theism. So Moyers makes this statement and asks a powerful question—he says "I'll tell you what the most gripping scripture in the Christian New Testament is for me: 'I believe. Help thou my unbelief.' I believe in this ultimate reality, that I can and do experience it. But I don't have answers to my questions. I believe in the question: 'Is there a God?'"

Joseph Campbell wasted no time, and launched into a story about what he calls an amusing experience at the New York Athletic Club swimming pool, and a Catholic Priest he had just been introduced to. The Priest reclined on a lawn chair next to Campbell after he had had a swim, and struck up a conversation by asking "Mr. Campbell, are you a Priest?" Campbell said "No, Father." The Priest then asked if he was Catholic, to which Campbell responded "I was, Father." Then the Priest asked, and Campbell says it's interesting that he asked it this way, "Mr. Campbell, do you believe in a personal God?" Campbell responded "No Father." And the Priest replied, "Well, I suppose there is no way to prove by logic the existence of a personal God." Campbell replied, "If there were, Father, what then would be the value of faith?" The Priest stood up quickly, and said "Well Mr. Campbell, it's nice to have met you!"

I love that story! Reflecting on it afterwards, Campbell called it an illuminating conversation, because he saw that when this man, a Catholic priest, asked him about a personal God, Campbell thought that meant that he also then "recognized the possibility of an impersonal God, namely, a transcendent ground or energy, or a luminous consciousness that informs all things and all lives."

He went on to say that "we unthinkingly live by fragments of that consciousness, fragments of that energy" and that "the religious way of life is to live not in terms of the self-interested intentions of this particular body at this particular time, but in terms of the insight of that larger consciousness."[34] In other words, personal expressions of God are conditioned, limited, cultural, familial, and representative of a particular place and time. But a true sense of the divine transcends these expressions, and is a conscious mystery that connects all of us in a web of creation. That's a powerful and illuminating story!

We all spring from an eternal consciousness that we can never fully understand or explain through prescribed creeds and beliefs. We can only trust that it is there, and try to live our lives in accordance with that presence that we feel within us and around us. I guess that's why I have always loved the expression *Namaste*, a Sanskrit term that means something along the lines of "the divine in me recognizes the divine in you." Whatever our particular god is, on the personal, conditioned side, when we can break from that, and truly look at one another as though we possess a sense of the divine, we penetrate right through that

---

[34] Campbell/Moyers, 265-66

personal god to the heart of a luminous consciousness that we all hold in common. And great things can stem from that connection, *if* we can free ourselves to have that experience. And isn't that what Paul is saying, or at least what the writer of Luke is telling us Paul said, when he wrote, "we all live, and move, and have, or share our being *in* God"? Paul does not say God is out there, distant, but is rather the foundation of our life, our breath, and is never far from each one of us.

Paul may struggle, as he appears to, with the idea of God as unknowable, preferring concrete images instead, but he is definitely inching into the mystical realm in denouncing belief in a God who lives in shrines and is served by humans, the hallmarks of supernatural theism. He is, or perhaps Luke, the author of Acts is, moving in the right direction here, for to see God as the ground in which we live and move and share our being, well, that changes everything, and throws supernatural theism right out the window.

To have faith that we share our being in God is to let the mystery flow through us as we accept the invitation into the realm of the experiential, where belief becomes inadequate, and where believing in things about God becomes uninspiring.

In the end, it's about experiencing the presence of the divine that the mystics have been talking about, where answers and systems and doctrines and dogma are simply unnecessary and woefully inadequate, as compared to opening oneself to the mystery of this thing we call "God" and basking in that presence within and around us. How did Hildegard of Bingen put it? She said something like "the mystery of God hugs you in its all-encompassing forms." I like that.

When we can put aside the God of supernatural theism, when we can trust, as faith calls us to do, that "God" is the mysterious reality in which we live, then we open ourselves to a whole new way of living in this world together as one, unified in a creative essence, regardless of our differences. And through this oneness, a new sense of community will blossom. That's what's at stake here friends, as we leave the diety of old behind, and open ourselves to the intimacy and mystery that Jesus so often spoke of. It's only scary for a little while. . . I promise.

Going back ever so briefly to that Pew Research Poll and the idea of the Nones, when I got the call yesterday telling me that my 49-year-old sister Sue had died, I remember thinking that she was one of those 23 percent who would be described as a "None." She left all of this religious stuff a long, long time ago and never felt a need to go back. Yet as I spent time talking with her as she was just days from dying when I made my last visit, I realized how deeply spiritual she was, and how she had no need of certainty or answers about where her journey was taking her. She just had this deep sense of peace and trust, call it faith, that she was in the midst of a community in which "we live and we die and death not ends it," to quote one of her favorites, Jim Morrison.

I'll never forget our final words during my last visit to her bedside. She put her hand up, looked into my eyes with this confident and peaceful smile on her lips, and said, "See you on the other side." And I put my hand on hers and said, "See you on the other side." And then she went peacefully to sleep, that gentle smile still on her lips.

On my flight home, I realized that all the theology, all the rules, all the judgment, all of the ideas of a god choosing some and not others, all of the certainties, all of the wrath, all of the rewards and punishments of the supernatural god in the sky, all of that stuff just falls woefully short of capturing the essence of life, or of death. It fails to define the amazing mystery that we live, and move, have our being, and ultimately die within, as my sister did just a few days later, and as so many of your own loved ones have done before you as well.

And I thought to myself, this mystery-of-God thing is so much more awesome than anything we can imagine, or take from a book written and compiled long ago. I learned that lesson fully in those last couple of days with my sister, and as I look back on it, it's been nothing short of a breathtaking realization loaded with spiritual freedom and confidence in the holiness of each of our personal travels through life and beyond. And what we have been naming 'God' is woefully inadequate to accompany us on the awesomeness of our journeys. For they are not journeys to be believed in, but rather to be experienced.

I want to end this sermon with the words of Mystic Meister Meister Eckhart, as interpreted by Matthew Fox: "God is not found in the soul by adding anything, but by a process of subtraction." Subtraction and letting go leads us to the Divine depths. When we can let go and "sink into God," amazing things happen between God and us. "I advise you to let your own 'being you' sink into and flow away into God's 'being God.' Then your 'you' and God's 'his' will become so completely one 'my' that you will eternally know with him his changeless existence and his nameless nothingness."[35]

Find a way to sink into the mystery of "God" this week in a new way, and I think you will be astounded by the experience. Leave the belief at the door, and accept the invitation to fully experience the presence of God where you truly live and move and have your being. Namaste and Amen.

Sermon #4 - The Bible

Scripture - *Numbers 6: 24-28; Micah 6:8; Psalm 139: 14-18; Matthew 6: 25-27 & Matthew 22: 37-40*

One of my favorite things to do on Christmas Eve each year, when I get home after our evening service and everyone in my house has gone off to bed, is to turn on my TV and seek out the Midnight Mass broadcast from Rome. I know I have quite the exciting life! I love the pomp and pageantry of this special service celebrating the birth of Jesus. They know how to do it in style!

My favorite moment is when the Gospels are about to be read. If you have never witnessed this, you should check it out, because it is ceremonially fascinating. First, there are several readings by various lay people, from an ordinary Bible residing on the lectern. But then, after these readings, everyone turns and looks down the long nave of St.

---

[35] Matthew Fox, *Meister Eckhart, www.newworldlibrary.com*

Peter's Basilica. Dramatic organ music begins and drowns the space in sacred energy, and then you see a priest in flowing white robes emerging from a cloud of incense, with a book held high over his head.

He walks the length of the center aisle, as people bow and shed tears and as more incense is released into the already cloudy and fragrant basilica air. He reaches the front, and the organ music builds to a crescendo as the priest walks up the stairs to the altar where the Pope is waiting, and hands the book to His Eminence while everyone bows in reverence. The Pope then kisses the book containing the Gospels and lifts it high over his head, turning it each way to show it to the massive crowd. He lowers the book and opens it to the appropriate Gospel passage of Jesus' birth. He then places it carefully on the altar, right behind the very white, curly-haired, painted porcelain baby Jesus statue. If you have never seen this act, Christmas is right around the corner and it will be repeated soon. Make sure you check it out!

I was thinking of this ceremonial act this week as I was reflecting on the Bible and its place in our lives as Christians, and the unwavering reverence so many ascribe to it as a holy book: a book to never be questioned, a book to be read with great humility, a book that contains the very literal words and stories of God as many of us were taught growing up.

It is also a book, by the way, that you can find in just about any hotel room if you just open one of the dresser drawers. And if you ask most people to name one book on their bookshelf, I am guessing the Bible will come up as answer number one more often than not. You could follow that up by asking them how much dust is on that Bible from its having sat there so long without being opened as well!

Regardless of how long it has been since they have opened this book, there is no doubt they'll all stand proud in the fact that they have one. The Guinness Book of World Records, in fact, confidently declared this: "Although it is impossible to obtain exact figures, there is little doubt the Bible is the world's best-selling and most widely distributed book. A survey of the Bible Society concluded that around two and a half billion copies were printed between 1815 and 1975, but more recent estimates put that number at more than five billion."[36] That's a lot of Bibles! They also estimate that the Bible has been translated into over 350 languages, and that there are hundreds of different translations in English alone. And of course we know the place the Bible occupies in the minds of many, especially those who commonly fall under the umbrella of Fundamentalism: the Bible is *the* actual Word of God.

Ask any Fundamentalist Christian and they will tell you the Bible contains the literal truths of the acts of God in the world, from creation in six days to the great flood, to the story of the deliverance of Israel, to the virgin birth of Jesus and his salvific and atoning death on the cross. And of course it goes right through to Paul's letters and the founding of the church and finally to the second coming and the final things to come in Revelation. The Bible, for so many, is a factual recounting of God's words and deeds and promises, recorded long ago but timeless in scope, and it is to be lived by as the heart of one's faith and understanding of God generally without question.

I would guess that most of us here in the United Church of Christ (UCC) don't subscribe to the notion that the Bible is the "literal word of God," that randomly fell from the sky one day in King James format and hit someone in the head, or that angels were busy acting as divine messengers, going between God and busy secretaries on earth, dictating to them what God had said.

The UCC's unofficial motto is that "we take the Bible seriously, not literally", though admittedly even in some UCC churches this view of the Good Book has still not been fully embraced. In considering this ancient book as Progressive Christians we must ask ourselves what place the Bible should hold in our lives. How does it inform how we live as spiritual beings? How does it inspire us to follow this man named Jesus? How does it shape our understanding of our relationship to God? How does it cement us as a spiritual community? Some of you may answer quite simply: "It doesn't shape any of this—it's just a book of fairy

---

[36] *http://www.guinnessbookofworld'srecords.com*

tales." For others it might be the foundation of your faith, even though you do not take it literally. Some might avoid thinking about the Bible at all because it is so coated in verbal grime from historical misinterpretation and downright abuse over time. And for still others, it might just be flat out overwhelming to examine the Bible in any kind of contextual way in an attempt to understand its origins. I am sure right here in this place, we have a range of opinions on the Bible.

My own relationship to the Bible has shifted over time. When I was a kid growing up in a Lutheran Church, attending Sunday school and confirmation, I was never inspired by any of this Bible stuff. It all sounded like fairy tales and myths to me from the very beginning, and just didn't resonate with my life. I somehow muddled through confirmation, and after that I was free to decide whether I wanted to waste my time with church anymore. And so I left church, for at least a decade, swearing I was done with it for good. But eventually something drew me back, and it wasn't the magical stories and miracles of the Bible. Rather it was the poetry and justice and wisdom in the Bible. It was moving descriptions of the human condition. It was the all-too-human characters and their attempt to figure out where this mystery we name "God" was in the midst of their lives. In the words of Karl Barth, I "discovered a strange, new world within the Bible"[37] And it was a world I had never known before.

Like many of you, as I was growing up in the church, I was taught that the Bible tells the sweep of history from creation in six days in Genesis to the end of time in Revelation, and sandwiched in between were strange stories about arks and floods, men living in whales, burning bushes that spoke, talking donkeys, a whole lot of violence, anger, wrath and of course warnings about my sinful nature. I was taught that I should just believe all of this bible stuff as the core around which my spiritual life should unfold.

It wasn't until I started asking some hard questions, especially in seminary, that it all really started to come alive for the first time. For

---

[37] Barth, Karl, *The Word of God*, New York, NY: Harper & Brothers, 28.

instance, it was when I learned that the first five books of the Bible were not written by Moses, and that in fact Moses might never have even existed, that there is a real chance he is more like a character in a great story, a collage of hopes fashioned into a historical leader in a sense. Who knows? And I learned that the Older Testament, what our Jewish sisters and brothers call the Hebrew Scriptures, is the product of centuries of development. It contains all sorts of very different contexts and cultures mashed together to form a holistic picture of the journey of Israel and their collective experience of their God, whether it be Yahweh, Elohim, Adonai to name a few different names for God through the Hebrew Scriptures.

I learned that the Bible was not the work of God, but was rather the work of human beings over a long period of time. Ever wonder why there are two creation stories that are very different? Or why there are two different Ark stories intertwined together? Ever wonder where Cain's and Abel's wives came from? These are just a few examples of different sources telling and retelling stories and myths of deep meaning, which our tradition handed down to us over time as literal truths.

Then as I began to study the New Testament in detail, I realized that I had been misled my entire life into thinking the whole thing just flowed beautifully from Matthew, through the Gospels and the story of Jesus, to the beginning of the church in Acts, and then of course Paul's letters and other's writings, and finally concluding with what will happen in the end in Revelation. Friends, that's not remotely close to the truth! If you place everything in the New Testament in chronological order, the reality is that you come up with a very different picture. You have Jesus' life lived until around 35CE, give or take a few years; then Paul starts writing his letters to small communities around the year 50CE or so; and you have Paul's death in the 60's. There were no known Gospels when Paul was writing.

And then came the most important event for the development of our New Testament: the destruction of the Jewish Temple in the Roman-Judean war around the year 70CE, thirty-five years or so after Jesus' death. I cannot tell you how important this event was for the development of the Gospels and the New Testament. Because only then, in the smoldering ruins of the Temple, do you have the emergence of what we call a "gospel", meaning an account of the "good news". This Gospel was later called Mark. In the coming decades the gospels of Matthew and Luke were written, and finally much later came John's gospel. It was not until the end of the second century that those four we now call the Gospels began to be seen as central, mainly through the work of some powerful bishops, such as one named Irenaeus, who settled on the number four through this reasoning:

It is not possible that the Gospels can be either more or fewer in number than they are. For, since there are four zones of the world in which we live, and four principal winds, while the Church is scattered throughout the world, and the pillar and ground of the Church is the Gospel...it is fitting that she should have four pillars.

Biblical scholar Bart Ehrman sums his words up well, saying,

In other words—four corners of the earth, four winds, four pillars and necessarily, then, four Gospels.[38]

Yet even this is not the end, for the Bible as you know it was still almost two centuries away. In 367CE a man named Athanasius wrote down, for the first time in history, the twenty-seven books of the New Testament that we have today. Even that did not settle the matter, however, for the debate raged on and the New Testament would not officially be declared closed for several more centuries. And of course, we now know that there are many other books that have been discovered, named after Judas, Mary Magdalene, and Thomas just to name a few, that were never included in the biblical canon.

---

[38] Ehrman, Bart, *Misquoting Jesus*, 35

This book, in other words, from the Older Testament to the Newer, was a long-time and complex product made from human hands and imaginations, human hopes and dreams, human history and mythology, human fears and longings, human pain and ultimately the search for the experience of God in human life. Taking it literally is simply out of the question and, I will say, foolish. But that doesn't mean that we can't hold on to the great deal of beauty and "truth" that the Bible contains and find meaning within its stories and characters still to this modern day. I am reminded of what the late, great Marcus Borg was so fond of saying: "The Bible is true, and some of it actually happened."[39] There are truths in the Bible for sure, and it doesn't have to be historically literal for that to be the case.

So the question remains: What is the Bible to the Progressive Christian? Because we do not believe it is literally the Word of God, or even perhaps inspired by God in the sense of traditional Christianity, what does it mean to us? Can it still teach us something? Fred Plumer, the President of Progressivechristianity.org seems to think so. He answers that question this way:

> *In summary, what the Bible does do for us is that it gives us the right questions: how to live our lives, how to live together, how to form community, how to treat not only each other, but how to treat everything around us. It's a way of approaching our lives that may not give us the answers, but asks us, or provides for us questions to help us find the right answers that allow us to live together in harmony.*[40]

I like Plumer's words, and I know that when I go to the Bible and encounter a story about Jesus, whether or not it is historical, metaphorical, or a blending of the two, I find myself inspired to live my

---

[39] Borg, Marcus, *The Heart of Christianity*, 51

[40] *https://www.youtube.com/watch?v=zHFDepyaJqo*

life in a certain way geared toward what we think were his hopes and dreams for the world. We can take really powerful stuff from this book: the love and peace; the call to do justice and walk humbly; the call to notice the lilies of the fields, or the birds of the air; and the call to remember how easily sin, defined as estrangement or injustice, can intrude upon our lives and our hearts and how we need to take notice and turn from it. If we can live by these principles, then I am pretty sure we are on the right path in life and the Bible is doing exactly what it is supposed to be doing: guiding us on that journey in a spiritually healthy way.

In the end, my friends, the Bible isn't meant to be believed in; it is meant to be lived. It is not meant to be revered, but rather to be experienced. The Bible is not meant to be a step-by-step manual for how to live, but is intended to inspire us to new spiritual depths and remind us that we stand in a long line of seekers and spiritual beings. If we can approach the Bible in this way, then it can be a powerful force for good in our lives.

I have shared my experience of the Bible with you, and now I encourage you to think hard of your own experience and ask yourself what this ancient book means to you as a Progressive Christian. And remember, you don't have to believe in it literally; you don't have to throw it out the window either. You don't have to burn incense around it and carry it high over your head. You just have to "be not afraid" of it. If you can get to that point, I think you too will discover a strange, new, metaphorical world within its pages, and it will grasp you in an entirely new way than ever before. Amen.

Sermon #5 - Knockdown in Nicaea - The Trinity
Scripture - *Matthew 28: 16-20*

You've all heard of the famous battles throughout time: Hector/Achilles at Troy; Athens vs. Sparta; Ali/Frazier and the Thrilla in Manila; Cowboys/Packers in the Ice Bowl; Palmer vs. Nicklaus at the Masters;

Serena & Venus Williams at Wimbledon; and there are many more I am sure that you hold dear. But for a theological geek like me, there is one battle that raged over the course of sixty or more years that I love. It's a battle that was brutal and dangerous, resulting in exiles and excommunications, smack-downs in both the physical and intellectual sense, and all sorts of charges of heresy.

I am talking of the battle that began in the year 319/320 CE, and really took off on the date of May 10th, 325 CE, in the ancient city of Nicaea in Asia Minor. On this date, under the watchful eye of the Emperor Constantine himself, two men with opposing views, two bitter Christian enemies *(strange to say)* battled it out with everything they had, wielding their theological and philosophical assertions like sharp swords, hurling insults and accusations and shrewdly maneuvering alliances more efficiently than Frank Underwood in House of Cards! Of course, I am talking about the greatest battle that 99 percent of people have never heard of, yet one that affects the spiritual lives and views of God for the Christian faithful like nothing else. Ladies and Gentlemen, distinguished guests and dignitaries, I give you: The Knockdown in Nicaea!

In this corner, which we are calling the "Jesus *Sure is* God" corner, and representing the then-emerging views of Christian Orthodoxy, we find Bishop Alexander from Alexandria, a wise and calm sage, and his young assistant Athanasius, who at only nineteen years old is already a theological powerhouse. They have come to this city of Nicaea at the request of the Roman Emperor Constantine, to argue their side of the growing conflict that was spreading throughout Christian regions regarding the nature of Jesus in relation to God. Was Jesus always there with God from time eternal? Is Jesus of the same substance and therefore co-eternal with God, not a creation of God? Yes, yes and yes, argues Alexander and his school of budding Trinitarians. They will fiercely represent this side over the coming thirty days of lengthy and heated debate.

And in the opposite corner, which we are calling the "Jesus *Ain't* God" corner we have a man named Arius, and his chief fighter Bishop Eusebius of Nicomedia, a pit bull of a man known as a crafty and cunning advocate. These two men also traveled to Nicaea at the summons of the Emperor to attend what became known as the Council of Nicaea, the first gathering of its kind in Christian history. Arius and Eusebius are here to argue their side of this dispute over the nature of Jesus, trying to bring in more converts to their claim that, as their tag line goes: "there was a time when *he*, {Jesus}, was *not*." The Arians asserted that Jesus, as the Word of God, was a creature, though a higher form of created being than ordinary human beings, wrought by God as the first act of creation. They argued that Alexander's view, that Jesus was co-eternal with God, meant that there were two gods, and monotheism therefore was impossible. Jesus, in their view, was not God by nature, but was in a sense promoted by God from his creation, to become the Word of God within creation. To assert otherwise was to wander into the realm of polytheism. Against Alexander, they would argue this side passionately for the next thirty days.

Of course I am recounting this story today because today is what we call Trinity Sunday, the Sunday following Pentecost when the Church remembers not an event, but rather an idea or belief that some call the deepest and greatest mystery of Christian theology, and yet one that others call the greatest bunch of mumbo-jumbo made up by old men from long ago. And of course I am speaking of the Trinity, the doctrine they began to carve out at Nicaea over those thirty days, and one that took another sixty years to formally hammer out. It's a doctrine that some denominations cling to passionately today and bring into their worship service every week by reciting the Nicene Creed. Yet it's also a doctrine that other denominations seem almost embarrassed by, to the point where they have drafted their own creedal language to move away from this ancient concept of a Holy Trinity that many church leaders find hard to explain, and that many of their followers find equally hard to understand.

The United Church of Christ (UCC) falls in that latter spectrum, but even more so Unitarians and Unitarian Universalists, who flatly deny the Trinity as a part of their identity. But any way you look at it, the Trinity likely has a hold on every one of you here even at the most subconscious level, and it has unavoidably shaped your spirituality by filtering the scriptures through its complex tri-part existence for the past 1,700 years. You can try to deny it, but like that strange uncle that no one understands sitting in your living room at a family party—the one no one wants to have to get stuck by—it's always there.

To understand the Trinity, you really have to try to grasp the historical times that it emerged from, and especially the times that led to Constantine's convening that first-ever council. You need to remember that until Constantine's conversion and his act of making Christianity a legal religion, Christians were still being persecuted, harassed, tortured, and killed. And Christianity was fairly local in flavor, meaning it had quite striking and different ways of seeing things depending on where one was, and especially what language one was speaking. In the West it was Latin; in the East it was Greek.

But that all began to change when Constantine made Christianity the focal point of his new unified empire. He wanted Christianity to become the cement that held his vast empire together. As he surveyed Christianity, however, he noticed that was not the case, and so he sought for the first time in history to have the state—the political, secular power—intervene in hammering out Christian doctrine. And luckily for him, a little kerfuffle brewing in Alexandria, in Egypt, provided just the perfect opportunity for the state to interpose itself in what was otherwise a theological matter. The dustup goes back to the two gentlemen I introduced earlier: Arius, a priest, and his bishop, Alexander, and their intense disagreement over the nature of Jesus. As Karen Armstrong tells it, passion and frenzy overtook Alexandria and the surrounding areas over this issue. She wrote:

Sailors and travelers were singing versions of popular ditties that proclaimed that the Father alone was true God, inaccessible and unique, but that the Son was neither coeternal nor uncreated, since he received life and being from the Father.[41]

---

[41] Armstrong, Karen, *A History of God*, 107

She goes on to recount stories that we have today, of bath attendants, moneychangers and bakers getting in heated arguments over the nature of Jesus in relation to God, writing:

People were discussing these abstruse questions with the same enthusiasm as they discuss football today![42]

This topic was hot and it was spreading, and Constantine decided he had to solve this before he watched his imperial glue come undone. And so began the Knockdown at Nicaea...

Now, as fascinating as all of this is to me, I realize that this subject may just bore some of you to death, so for the sake of time, let's just say that the Council was called, and Constantine himself presided, even taking the title "Thirteenth Apostle" for himself. Over the next several weeks, our fighters literally went at it tooth and nail, intellectually as well as physically. There are stories of one of Arius's followers reading from a scroll, and having it slapped from his hand. There are legends of bishops punching one another, and of demands for charges of heresy, and for exile and ex-communication.

In the end, Alexander's and Athanasius' view that Jesus was eternal with God carried the day, and Arius' counter-argument that Jesus was created by God rather than co-eternal with God, had lost. The Council drafted a document to state this, which we now know as the Nicene Creed, which was signed by everyone but Arius, Eusebius, and one other brave follower under the watchful eye of the Emperor. The statement, a first draft, was a full repudiation of everything those three stood for. Listen to the language:

We believe in One God, the Father Almighty, maker of all things visible and invisible. And in one Lord Jesus Christ, the Son of God, the only-begotten of the Father, that is, from one substance of the Father, God of God, light of Light, true God of true God, begotten, not made, of one substance with the father, through whom

---

[42] Ibid, 107

all things were made, both in heaven and on earth, who for us humans and for our salvation descended and became incarnate, becoming human. He suffered and rose again on the third day, ascended to the heavens, and will come again to judge the living and the dead.

And then, almost like they forgot, they added the words, *and in the Holy Spirit.* I love that! I could write another sermon just on the Holy Spirit and how that Spirit and God and Jesus are each God but also only One God in three persons, but...come to think of it, that would probably take another whole book, and even then I'm not sure I could explain it.

Anyhow, just to stick it to Arius and his followers a little more, one more part was added to the Nicene Creed that goes right to the heart of their argument in strong condemnation:

But those who say that there was a time when He was not, and that before being begotten He was not, or that He came from that which is not, or that the Son of God is of a different substance or essence, or that He is created, or mutable, these the Catholic Church condemns.

With this statement, and almost unanimous agreement from the 300 or so bishops, The Knockdown in Nicaea came to a close. But even with all of this the matter did not end, and it would take another sixty years and the creative work of three theologians named Gregory of Nyssa, Basil and Gregory of Nazianzus, until the matter could finally be put to rest. Well, as much as it could, we should say. For they, more than any others pulled the Trinity out from the realm of the rational, as though we could understand this and explain it through reason, and landed it squarely in the realm of the mystical, where contemplation and meditation were the only way to enter its mystery. As Karen Armstrong again writes,

Ultimately, the Trinity only made sense as a mystical or spiritual experience; it had to be lived, not thought, because God went far beyond human concepts.[43]

With that thought, the Trinity as we know it was made official. I guess once we understand this history, and it is way more complicated than my little "cliff notes" version relayed here, we must ask ourselves what it all means today, for us, a spiritual community drinking deeply at the well of progressive theology. I am guessing most of you have a conflicting relationship with the Trinity as part of your spiritual life; trust me when I assure you that you are by no means alone in your doubts about this fundamental Christian doctrine. However, it's an important concept from our tradition that we should grapple with.

On the one hand, we could just jettison it, as a theory that was fabricated by men long ago about things that they couldn't possibly have any way of knowing. They "made it all up as they went along" one could say, speaking about things they could not possibly comprehend. We could even see it as dangerous in a sense, because the Nicene Creed and the Trinitarian dogma that it espouses has often been held over people as a litmus test for their faith. Churches all over the world, right this very minute in fact, are busy reciting its words as a demonstration of their adherence to the orthodoxy that it promotes as the *only*, and proper, way to be Christian. I have had people tell me that if you did not recite that creed, or if you questioned it, you should be kicked out of the church.

We could also see the Creed as dangerous because it obscures the prophet and teacher that we know Jesus *was* and turns him to an icon to be worshipped, rather than a living example to be followed and emulated. It's a long and strange road, after all, that leads from the itinerant Galilean Preacher and social justice rabble-rouser Jesus to the Christ that is coeternal with God, light from light, true God from true God. Believing in this idea then becomes the crux of our faith, rather

---

[43] Ibid, 117

than the path of experience that he called us to walk. Faith then becomes only a personal set of rules to follow, rather than a communal life to be shared and explored.

On the other hand, maybe, just maybe, there is some real depth and power to this idea of the Trinity. Not in the sense of believing that it is actually true and the way things are, but rather as a reminder that our relationship to God is always metaphorical and symbolic and mystical, that it is never concrete, and that there is deep meaning in that. God is beyond anything we have language for, and therefore indescribable other than by names we create like God, or Holy One, or Great Mystery, or Yahweh, or Allah or whatever, all metaphors for something that we cannot understand.

Yet at the same time, the feeling of distance created by that recognition is counterbalanced by the sense that this mystery called God, which seems unapproachable, is also fully a part of us, burning deep within us as the very ground of our being as spirit, closer than the beat of our own hearts or the breath we take. Perhaps we can create our own version of the Trinity to help explain our relationship to God through a threefold process: First, recognizing the awe and wonder of what we experience as God, and the peace and fullness we feel in that moment; second, understanding that, through that awe and wonder, something amazing is present within and around us that is greater than ourselves; and finally, manifesting the love that emerges from that awe and wonder into the world through acts of compassion and justice as Jesus did. If that's the meaning we can take from this ancient and confusing concept, then I think it's a wonderful way to imagine and live the spiritual life. Don't take it literally and recite it. Rather live it and live your life by it, and the rest will all fall into place.

I know this sermon was a bit complicated. How can anything about as lofty and bizarre a concept as the Trinity be otherwise, right? But it's good that we encounter and explore the Trinity, because as a progressive, Protestant church, I often worry that we teeter on the verge of complete and utter rationalism, and have a tendency to lose sight of the mystical, which the Trinity really attempts to speak to.

But I happen to think that spiritual maturity requires a bit of both. It requires a willingness to use our minds to filter out religious agendas and corruptions and falsities, yet it also requires a willingness to *not* live always in a world of logic and reason, but to allow ourselves to remain open to the mystical reality that God, our Ground of Being, must be in the end. For that is, after all, where we find Jesus. That is the heart of living his words to love and experience God; to love and experience ourselves as spiritual beings; and finally, to love and experience our neighbor in the same way. This is fascinating and meaningful stuff, if we are willing to journey into it honestly, contextually and mystically. Amen.

Sermon #6 - From Galilee to God: An Honest Image of Jesus

Scripture - *1ˢᵗ Corinthians 11: 14-16 and 15: 3-8 & Matthew 26: 47-50*

In a previous sermon in this series on Progressive Christianity, I took you on a little journey back in time to the fourth century, more specifically to the years between 320 CE and 325 CE, into the midst of a brewing controversy that was getting really hot in certain areas of the newly-Christian Roman Empire. To recap briefly, the recently crowned Emperor Constantine had proclaimed religious tolerance for Christians in and around his empire. This was known as the Edict of Milan, from the year 313 CE. He did this not because he underwent some sort of conversion himself, but rather because he saw a political opportunity to use Christianity, which was spreading rapidly, as a sort of cement or glue to hold his vast empire together. But a major fight broke out among powerful Christian leaders in Alexandria, in Egypt, over the nature of Jesus as the Christ, and especially, as God.

Putting it simply, the question was this: had Jesus always been God eternally or was he created once upon a time? As we have seen, Constantine called the Council of Nicaea in 325 CE to settle this matter, and the result, after several weeks of intense battle, was that the Nicene

Creed was drafted to declare that Jesus was indeed coeternal with God and was therefore not created 'once upon a time.' The Nicene Creed also laid out and codified, for the first time, the concept of the Trinity. And by the year 381 CE, this Trinity formula would be about as complete as it will ever be. Many of you likely know it by heart, and have recited it over and over in your church traditions throughout your spiritual lives.

Studying the Trinity for that sermon really got me thinking about Jesus and his rather miraculous transformation from this itinerant, rural preacher from a small backwater town called Nazareth to the full-blown Son of God, the Messiah or the Christ, and eventually the second person of the Trinity: coeternally God, true God from true God, one in being with the Father, who will come again to judge the living and the dead.

I don't know about you, but to me that seems like one incredible journey! It seems quite fantastic—in fact, a little too fantastic! And if we fill out the picture of Jesus and the other amazing things that were told over time about him: that he was born of a virgin; that he performed miracles and brought people back from the dead; and that he was killed and was resurrected and ascended to God the Father; well then, we have the heart of what most would call the Christian story.

But the problem is that, increasingly, this story is being questioned. Thanks to the last hundred or so years of Jesus scholarship, and historical work on the context of Jesus' life and times and the first few centuries of the Christian movement before Constantine, many people have begun to doubt and question the story of Jesus' amazing life and his journey from Jesus to the Christ. So the time has come for us to take an honest look at Jesus, and leave our pre-conceptions and beliefs at the door. For I contend that only through losing Jesus as we have been taught to understand him, will we actually find him, as Marcus Borg says "for the first time."[44] But in a whole new way.

I first want to explore a couple of key ideas to letting go of a lot

---

[44] Borg, Marcus, *Meeting Jesus*, 3

of the Jesus Christ baggage that we have been carrying since we were kids in Sunday school, when we were initiated into the fanciful stories of the one we call Jesus Christ. First is the title Jesus carries: Christ. Now ask most people Jesus' name and they will answer "Jesus Christ." Some will even answer Jesus H. Christ, the H standing for God knows what. (I used to hear my Dad say this all the time, usually when he would hurt himself doing yard work or working on the car. "Jesus H. Christ!" he would yell!). Let's be clear here today that Christ is *not* Jesus' last name, nor is it a natural part of his name. Christ is a title. It is actually *Christos*, a Greek word that means "Anointed One." It is a translation of the Hebrew word *Messiah*, coming from the Jewish religious context that Jesus grew and lived within.

The Messiah, it is important to understand, was/is a hope for the Jewish people, as one who would some day rise up, like King David, to vanquish Israel's enemies and restore Israel to the heights of its glory. The Messiah would establish a reign of peace on earth for all time. As the church began to be increasingly formed in Greek terms and became separated more fully away from the Judaism from which it emerged, "Christos" became more infused with Jesus as a core part of his identity. That is so important to understand: Christ is a title.

The second Jesus idea we need to be reminded about is the fact that Jesus—and I'm going to shock many of you perhaps—was *not* a white dude! And he was especially not a white dude with long, flowing sandy brown hair and blue eyes. If you are like me, this is the Jesus you grew up with, the one you were called to worship and believe in, and this popular depiction of Jesus still lingers in the minds of many people today. In fact, I went to "Google Images" as I often do for Power Point images, and I searched for depictions of Jesus. I figured I would quickly find all sorts of diversity in this modern day and age. But this was not to be. I literally had to scroll through hundreds of images before I found a depiction of Jesus that might fit into the context of his Middle Eastern heritage two millennia ago.

So still today, the general conception is that Jesus was a white male. But it's time that we acknowledge the fact that *that* Jesus is just a fantasy, and more than that, a creation of the great European Renaissance and Baroque artists who interpreted him through their own cultures and contexts. A figment of our collective imagination. All sorts of cultures have done that, as it's pretty common to envision him through the cultural eyes of which one is a part. But doing so can also be dangerous, for then Jesus becomes like one of "us," and different than everyone else. And that creates a norm that has been the source of all sorts of issues over time.

Think no further than the history of slavery, for instance, which saw a white Jesus adopted by white culture against other peoples of the world, who were then devalued as sub-human chattel. This kind of religious white supremacy is dangerous still to this day. So it is important, as we try to see Jesus anew, that we do so honestly. And that means locating him as he was: a middle-eastern Jewish man, with a darker shade of skin, short hair, and likely shorter in stature than we envision today. And to envision Jesus this way is nothing short of a beautiful thing!

In fact, the scriptures for today's service (1st Corinthians 11: 14-16 and 15: 3-8, and Matthew 26: 47-50) confirm this for us. Look at First Corinthians, for example, and Paul's words about hair length. Paul says:

If a man wears his hair long, it is degrading for him.

Yet in this same letter, Paul says that he himself had a vision of Jesus. So did Jesus disgrace himself with the long, flowing hair that we envision him with? Not likely. And then take our text from Matthew. Let me ask you a question: if Jesus was a six foot five inch white, European male with long flowing hair, do you really think Judas would have to identify him with a kiss so they could arrest him? Come on! Jesus fit the mold of a Middle Eastern Jewish man as would be typical of his context, plain and simple.

To help explain this further, I want to share the story of what a team of medical artists and forensic archaeologists did a few years ago when it came to changing how we see Jesus.[45] This team wanted to create an image of a typical man from the region where Jesus lived, to determine as accurately as they could what Jesus *might have* actually looked like. So they acquired three well-preserved skulls from Jerusalem, from men who likely would have been around 30-33 years old. Through precise measurements and computer modeling of muscles, bone structure, skin and features, and using all available physical evidence of human bodies from people in this region at this time, they arrived at what they believed a typical Semitic, Middle Eastern man would look like.

And what they came up with created quite a stir, as the image of the man they created didn't fit what people had believed all their lives. Jesus was darker skinned, with curly, short black hair and beard. And keep in mind, they admitted openly that this was *not* the face of Jesus, but they believed firmly that it was close to what he would have looked like, as this would have been consistent with other skeletal findings from the area.

So, as I see it, the image created by these scientists and artists is the start of the Jesus story, in the context in which he lived. The story begins with a man who looked a lot like other Middle Eastern men of his time, who was born into Jewish culture in a small town in the region of Galilee, and was raised, along with his brothers and sisters, in the Jewish faith of his ancestors under the oppressive power of the Roman Empire.

At some point Jesus was baptized by a radical preacher called John the Baptist, and after John was killed, Jesus picked up John's passion and message and began traveling and preaching about what he called the Kingdom of God to the poor and downtrodden. He gathered quite a following, likely large crowds, and he began attracting attention by those whose responsibility it was to keep the peace at all costs. He caused a stir in Jerusalem, and he was eventually arrested and executed

---

[45] Fallon, Mike, *The Real Face of Jesus*: Popular Mechanics, January 23, 2015. *http://www.popularmechanics.com/science/health/a234/1282186/*

for sedition.

After his death, some believed that Jesus appeared to them, and a movement sprang up, carried forward by his brother James and his closest followers. Finally a man named Saul had some kind of vision and conversion, so the story goes, and Saul, or "Paul" as he became known, dedicated his life to founding small communities of Jesus followers, writing letters to them which we call Epistles. As these early "Christian" communities spread far and wide, some attempted to write the Jesus story for themselves, and the Gospels were born: first Mark, then Matthew and Luke and eventually John. Many other stories were written as well, that were not placed in the developing biblical canon.

And by the time we get to John, likely written in the early second century, Jesus has had a bit of a makeover, having been transformed from this preaching prophet and teacher with a message of good news, to the Word, or the Logos of God. And then by the time we get to Nicaea, Jesus has become God in all fullness and wholeness, coeternal with God the Father, who came into the world to die to save believers from their sins. This is the journey from Jesus, a peasant minister, to the Christ, one in being with the eternal God. And that, my friends, is quite a journey!

As I prepared this sermon, I kept asking myself why, aside from the fact that Jesus is probably *the* major figure in the history of the world, am I telling you all of this? Besides being a teaching sermon of sorts, what do I hope this historical examination of Jesus and his transformation will provide for you, and how will all of this enhance your spiritual life? And then I thought to myself, why did Marcus Borg write his groundbreaking book "*Meeting Jesus Again for the First Time*," that was read by millions of Christians seeking greater meaning in their lives? Or why did John Shelby Spong write "*Why Christianity Must Change or Die*," a provocative book that was also read by millions of people?

And then it hit me: it's because we, as Christians, are hungering for a spirituality that we can really live within, that isn't a source of embarrassment. It's because we are feeling suffocated by a stagnant faith from millennia ago that is all about believing in unreal and mythical things, as well as judgmental creations that are just not relevant any more in our modern times. It's because we want to move beyond belief and into the domain where our spirituality is alive and flowing in our daily lives, calling us to experience this mystery we call God. People are starving for that experience!

And I thought, if people don't have an honest encounter with the Christian faith we were raised within, and which we have come to realize is more mythic and make-believe than it is real, then we will just remain stuck, and we will continue to go through the motions of a religious way of life that is neither honest nor inspiring. We will remain far removed from a spiritual life that is exhilarating and full of awe and wonder as our encounter with this mystery we name God *should* be! And the visible results of that lack of honesty are rapidly declining church membership, the loss of thousands of churches being sold off to developers each year, and increasing secularism and the slow death of a stagnant faith, leaving a spiritual void that leads us to just give up on spirituality all together.

But even more important than all of that is the fact that without an honest look at our faith, and without a renewed way to enter into it, the needed and vital message of the historical Jesus is being lost right along with all of those churches. His prophetic and mystical message of the Kingdom of God being among us is lost; his call to love our neighbor as ourselves is lost; his words of hope and justice for the suffering are lost; his message to live deeply into the world and into the heart of the mystery of God is lost. And that is a tragedy for our world. So we need to save it, and part of that means knowing honestly how it all developed, so we can reclaim what it really was in the beginning and spread that word far and wide: that the true meaning of the Christian life is not about a system of beliefs to be followed, nor is it primarily a call to a moral code to be lived; it is rather a life of yearning and reaching for God just as Jesus did, with a vision of the world that can bring about the realities of harmony, love and peace.

In the end we should see that the journey from Jesus to the Christ doesn't end in Nicaea with lofty theological assertions. No way.

The journey from Jesus to the Christ is still ongoing, and every day it continues right here in our midst. Do something for me: point to yourself. Say "I am the Christ." Point to your neighbor, and say "you are the Christ." Now point to your neighbor and yourself at the same time, and say "we are the Christ together." Now hold up your hands, and say with me "these are the hands of Christ." Now point your feet, and say with me "these are the feet of Christ." And finally, point to your heart, and say with me "this is the heart of Christ."

Congratulations! You just reclaimed an honest faith, and summed up the Christian life, and it is alive in you and all around you right this very moment. Now let's stop believing in it, and let's go live it and experience it. And through those experiences I guarantee you, we will meet and experience Jesus like we never thought was possible before. Amen.

Sermon #7 - Death and the Afterlife

Scripture - *1st Corinthians 15: 51-55*

I wonder how many of you keep a bucket list, a list of things you want to do and experience in your life before you are "called up to the big leagues", so to speak. I am guessing many of you do. I know I do. One big experience that is on my list is to spend a few days in Mexico during what is known as *Dia de los Muertes*, or the "Day of the Dead." The purpose of this multi-day fiesta celebration is to remember those loved ones who have died and passed on to the other side, and invite their spirits back to share in the feast.

This colorful and creative festival has its origins among the indigenous people of Mexico who, beginning on what is for us Halloween and continuing through the next Wednesday, celebrate the memory of their beloved ones who have left this mortal world before them. They build creative altars of mementos, bake ceremonial foods, dress up in colorful costumes, throw lavish parties and parades, and feast together, all with the hope of rejoining their dear departed ones in spirit for this short time.

The decorated altars dedicated to loved ones are an important part of the festivities. Some are very small, like little shoebox-sized dioramas, while others are massive, complex and busy displays of love, yet all are colorful and celebratory of the life whose loss they are lamenting and whose spirit they hope will be drawn back for a brief visit. I love this celebration, and I long to be part of it someday.

I wanted to invite you into the experience of *Dia de los Muertes* and these lavish, colorful celebrations of departed loved ones because I see this ancient ceremonial practice, which goes back in some estimations to 3,000 BCE, as a deeply meaningful and powerfully hopeful way to engage the death process, the one thing that touches all of us in one way or another. What is that old saying? There are only two certainties in life: death and taxes? Death will strike us all by taking ones we love, and eventually enveloping our own lives in that final farewell. This is just a fact we cannot escape no matter how hard we might try. Yet, in the Day of the Dead celebrations I see so much hope manifest: hope that we will commune with our loved ones again; hope that we will feel their spirits and their continuing presence in our lives; and finally, hope that we will join them again when we ourselves die and take the journey deeper into the mystery of God, in whom we live and move and share our being.

Celebrations like this instill in me the confidence that death is just a transition, a doorway, a moving-on from our physical life on earth into a bigger universe, and a final chance to leave a legacy of love and peace to those who carry on the great work of being human. There is no fretting in these celebrations, although Catholic missionaries tried hard to instill as best they could notions of heaven and hell, punishment and reward, comfort and misery into these cultures and celebrations. But at their core, as they are still practiced with ancient nuances, they simply and beautifully reflect the journey that we are all on: that we live, we die, but death does not end it.

Today's service is about remembering our loved ones, our own saints who have passed on into new life, yet it is also a day, given the fact that we are still in the midst of this Progressive Christianity series, to examine how our own tradition sees death and the afterlife. And unfortunately, many of us Christians have been conditioned to experience death *only* in terms of Christian theology, where it has been turned into a judgmental system of rewards and punishments. We are either going to be saved or damned, and the afterlife is dangled like a prize in front of us to be awarded for holding to the right beliefs, or living the right kind of life as laid out within our changing religious tradition. If we participate in certain religious events or practices, we will find salvation and see our loved ones again in this next life that we have earned. If we do not follow those rules, we risk swimming in rivers of fire for all eternity and will never be "saved".

I think this is unfortunate, and I will in fact argue that the idea of salvation in this sense is the greatest crime and sin ever perpetrated on humanity. This idea that we need salvation has robbed death of its depth and stripped it of any notion of being an intimate part of the human condition. Dying then becomes about power exercised by a narrow, controlling religion. Our fear of death becomes a fear of living, as we question whether we are to be saved or damned, and as our lives and beliefs are dictated by those who somehow know the will of God and who have the awesome power of heaven or hell to back up their claim. It is, and I can't think of a better way of putting it, complete and utter garbage, and it's time we threw this ghastly idea into the theological garbage dump.

When we are free to use our minds, and really think about it, humanity in general has been in the stage of evolution that scientists label "Homo Sapiens" on this earth for only about 200,000 years. The Church, and its notion of salvation as necessary for the experience of a good afterlife, has only been around for about 1600 years, give or take a few decades. Think about that! That means for roughly 198,400 years, people lived and they died, and they did so in times when there was no original sin to save them from, no Church to judge them, no Jesus Christ who takes away the sins of the world and no Christian merits for the afterlife. This is so important to remember when thinking about the journey that is death. Christianity only owns one tiny fraction of time in which our human consciousness has existed, and therefore owns very little of the death experience itself.

Do you ever ask yourself, as I do any time I encounter a theological assertion, how did we arrive at a particular conclusion or place? In our case today, how did our death experience come to be filtered through the lens of Christian theology, through sin and salvation, and through Jesus Christ as the only path to heaven? Those are fascinating and important questions for us to wrestle with. And luckily for us, what we find is actually an easily traceable historical timeline for the development of ideas about what happens when one dies.

For starters, one way to explore this is to go way back into ancient cultures and contexts, such as Egyptian culture, which had this idea that when one died, they had to travel to the underworld and face trials and gatekeepers in order to reach the god Osiris, in front of whom they would plead their case for entry into the afterlife. First they stood in front of what was known as the "42 divine judges." That's Part One. Part Two involved a weighing of the heart against what they told the judges. The heart was a record of all one did in their lifetime. If the scales balanced, they were then granted eternity in what was called the *Field of Rushes,* where life resumed pretty much as it had before they died. And for those who didn't pass the test? They fell into the hands of demons and received eternal torment. Sound familiar?

The Greeks, in their earliest history, had of course many gods and goddesses, one of them being Hades, the brother of Zeus and Poseidon. Hades was the god of the underworld, where *all* mortals went when they died. Hades was just kind of a place to hang out for all eternity, a gloomy place probably akin to detention for your average high school student! As Greek civilization developed and evolved, of course so did the afterlife, and it dawned on the Greeks that not *everyone*, especially not the great thinkers and heroes, should have to dwell in Hades. So, the concept of the Elysian Fields evolved over time, a place where the rich and famous go: the philosophers, the athletes, the poets, basically the elite of Greek society and culture. Life was grand in the Elysian Fields, where, according to Homer, "life is easiest for the men," and according to Hesiod, "they live untouched by sorrow."

Judaism, from which Christianity emerged, had no real concrete beliefs of an afterlife. The Pharisees believed in a general resurrection of the dead to come; the Sadducees did not. Some Talmudic sects of Judaism, however, did believe in what they called "The World to Come", where the righteous enjoy a lavish eternal existence according to how they lived during their lives. Others, those who did not live so righteously, descended to a place called "Gehenna", where for a period not to exceed twelve months they were punished. After twelve months, they assume their place in "The World to Come". Only the ultra-wicked were punished the whole 12 months, and then their souls were either destroyed or they lived on in an eternal state of remorse.

As far as the Bible goes, the *first-ever* reference to resurrection, to final judgment and the afterlife comes from the book of Daniel. Daniel is a strange, apocalyptic book that was written anywhere between 6th century BCE and the 2nd century BCE. And Christianity of course emerged out of this milieu and preached a strong message of general resurrection and eternal life for those who believed in Jesus Christ until around the 10th or 11th century of the common era, when in the misery of the middle ages, judgment took center stage, purgatory entered the scene and one's life-after-death experience was squarely at the mercy of an increasingly powerful religious structure and the rules that were conjured up by its powerful practitioners. Hell, in this time of the High Middle Ages, became very real and very awful.

Things began to change, however, as Martin Luther nailed his ninety-five Theses to the church door at Wittenburg in October of the year 1517. Luther struggled all his life as a priest with judgment and hell, and finally had enough when a certain man named Johan Tetzel came to his town selling indulgences, a monetary payment that could lessen a loved one's time in purgatory and curry favor with God to get them to eternal life in Heaven. "*A Coin in the coffer rings, a soul from purgatory springs*" was Tetzel's line, and the poor handed over coins that might have fed their families for a week to save their tormented loved ones from sitting for eternity in this place called purgatory.

With Luther, then, things began the slow process of changing, as his expanded idea of grace and faith began to cool some of the fires of fear that hung dangerously around the reality of death. Hell began to lose some of its power as the Protestant faith expanded, though it did not disappear altogether, and in more fundamentalist sects still burns strongly to this day.

I wanted you hear the Cliff Notes version of this history of beliefs about death and the afterlife because, like all theological assertions about God, it has a traceable lineage that has been filtered through the lenses of the experiences of various cultures and times, one strongly influencing and building on and adapting from another. And these experiences all culminate right here with us today, in this church, as we still live our lives under this ancient religious paradigm. In fact, the death experience for us is still being filtered through this history and any kind of "life after death" experience is still held captive to these ancient beliefs. And I think that is hugely unfortunate to our spiritual journeys and the transformation that awaits us when we ultimately pass into death as so many of our loved ones have before us.

I chose Paul's words about death today because I have a like/dislike relationship with them when it comes to death and what awaits us after. I think Paul got himself a little caught up in the glories of resurrection hysteria when he inked this letter to the community at Corinth, as he believed Jesus' second coming was imminently upon him in his time. So we take him with a grain of salt here, but I still think he was onto something.

As many of you know, I just lost my sister to death, a 49-year-old vibrant spirit who died from cancer way too young. I can tell you, and most of you know this from your own experiences, that death *freakin'* stings. It stings and wounds and it cuts deep into our humanity and alters us at the core of who we are as human beings. Where is death's sting, Paul asks? I'll tell you where. It's in every moment that you hear your deceased beloved's favorite songs; it's when a quiet memory of them slips into your mind when you are daydreaming; it's when families get together for the first time after a death and someone is missing; it's those first holidays; it's those special days that you used to share together. So "O Death where is your sting?" It lives in the heart of each moment! It's real and it's there and it's raw. Death stings. How can it not?

But, if you stay with this text from Paul a little while, you begin to see something else in what he is saying. He is actually quoting the Prophet Hosea with those words. Hosea is talking about restoration, in this case of Israel in a dark time of death and misery, and how out of death comes the reality of something new. Paul calls it mystery; he calls it change; he calls it transformation. He says "Let me tell you a mystery: we will not die, but we will be changed!" His language gets a little flowery and he is a theological person of his own time, but add these words to his other words about how we "live and move and share our being *in* God," and you begin to see that he was taking a radically new and strangely progressive step out of the religious beliefs about death that were common during that time.

In fact Paul never, once, anywhere, mentions Hell. Go look for it. You won't find it. He only speaks of death as life transformed and he speaks of how now we see dimly, but someday we will see clearly. He knows we don't have the answer to life after death, and he knows that death hurts, yet he stands confident that when we die, we will be transformed. And when we die, we die into this mystery that we call God. And that is nothing short of breathtaking.

That's what Progressive Christianity needs to be claiming today! We, as progressive Christians, need to proclaim that the old paradigm of sin and salvation and reward and punishment no longer useful or meaningful, and that death and the "what's next" of what awaits us after death is so much richer an experience than our religions have built for us. In fact, when people ask me if I believe in life after death I answer "absolutely!" Yet it's nothing like what we've been sold. I believe in it more like the author Henry Miller does, when he wrote "of course you don't die, nobody dies. Death doesn't exist, you only reach a new level of vision, a new realm of consciousness, a new unknown world."

I believe in life after death like our Native American friend White Eagle does, who wrote: "You live on earth only a few short years, which you call an incarnation. And then you leave your body like an outworn dress, and go for refreshment in your true home in the spirit." I believe in the afterlife like Kahlil Gibran does, who wrote: "When the earth shall claim your limbs, then you shall truly dance!"

Finally, I believe in an afterlife of energy, and in particular the animating spirit that makes us unique, is never destroyed, yet does live on to dance and reconnect with the mystery of God into which we live and have our being. I guess that's why the Day of the Dead celebration strikes me so deeply and why I want to experience it. For in that festive ritual I see the path to letting go of the theological baggage around death and dying, and opening ourselves to the trust that this is just a natural part of the journey of life that we will all take at some point, and that there is nothing to fear, and finally that our loved ones who have traveled ahead into death before us are okay. They are transformed in Spirit, dwelling more deeply in the God experience and still connected to us in ways that we cannot remotely understand in this time. I need not say or believe anything more than this, and I think I can even begin to say with Paul, "O Death, where is your sting?" Amen.

Sermon #8 - Expanding Into the Living Ether - Prayer
Scripture - *First Kings 19: 4-13; On Prayer, by Kahil Gibran*

To help prepare this final sermon of our series on Progressive Christianity, I looked back at some my past sermons about prayer to see how my views on the subject have changed over time. I quickly saw that I had said, on more than one occasion, that prayer is one of the most difficult topics that progressive Christians struggle with. And upon further reflection, I can state unequivocally today that I have not changed my opinion of that belief! Prayer, for the progressive Christian, is a tough topic!

As I looked back over my old sermons, I noticed that I spent a lot of time talking about how prayer should *not* be practiced according to the teachings of Progressive Christianity. I often described how we now know so much about the cosmos and scientific causes of events in our lives that the old supernatural "God in the Sky" theism is no longer a viable way to frame our spirituality, especially when it comes to prayer. That was the easy part. What I didn't say much about, however, was the much more difficult topic of just what prayer *is*. What meaning might prayer have in our lives if there is no God up there in the clouds to answer our prayers or to pray to? What's the point of prayer? These are the questions I want to focus on today.

As I continued working on this sermon, the topic of prayer was on many people's minds as a major storm, in this case Hurricane Matthew, was devastating parts of Florida and the Caribbean, especially the people of Haiti. And so the opportunity to think about prayer under the threat of this natural disaster was powerfully present, especially given the number of times people in the affected and threatened areas were described in news reports and on social media as "praying to God" to keep their area safe from destruction and harm. This is very natural.

As the worst of Matthew stayed offshore, I heard people proclaiming that God had protected them, or their property, or their city: "Thank you God!" they would say confidently, certain that God had heard their prayers and kept them and their property safe. This gratitude for being spared from harm through prayer was mainly expressed by people in Florida, who had apparently escaped major damage from the storm through the requested divine intervention.

Over the following days, as I heard these prayers of joy, I thought about the poor people of Haiti, who got absolutely crushed by this hurricane as the worst of it passed right through their country. Hundreds of Haitians were killed, and these people, who were already some of the world's poorest, were reduced to even more grinding poverty because of the storm. I asked myself sarcastically, in light of the traditional interventionist prayer paradigm: Where was God for the people of Haiti? Did they not pray enough? Did they not say the right kinds of prayers? Are they not the right kinds of Christians, or unfortunately for them, not Christian at all? Why did God not hear their prayers the way many believe God heard the prayers of those in Florida? And with that thought, this sermon on prayer was born!

For this lesson, I want to examine where prayer fits in with something the great theologian Karl Rahner once wrote: "The Christian of the future will be a mystic, or he (or she) will not exist at all." That's a provocative statement about the future of Christianity, and it really fits in well with Progressive Christianity because that is precisely the kind of statement progressive Christians would and should make about the topic of prayer. As we move into a new and unfolding spiritual future, with all the modern knowledge that we possess, and with a vastly different and more complex way of conceiving the world than existed in biblical times, we can surely see that our view of the function of prayer *must* evolve with us.

As we exit the realm of theism, which envisions a deity in the sky directly controlling things and events here on earth, this means that we need to stop praying to this omnipotent being as though he/she/it will actually protect us from all danger, heal all illness, make us rich and successful, or grant any wish we may desire. This is a distortion of the heart of what prayer should be about, not to mention a distortion of the meaning of "God". This idea belongs to an ancient practice whereby priests would sacrifice animals to gods to appease them, and through which the people, mediated through the priestly class, could then offer up their needs and desires for the sake of whatever god was answering the prayer or intercession. Petitioning a supernatural being in the heavens to change things for this or that reason, is just not a helpful or healthy way to enter into prayer anymore. And it's time we just admit that and stop deluding ourselves.

Prayer actually has so much more to offer! Prayer can take us into spiritual depths we have never experienced; prayer can change us at the core of our being and connect us in ways we have never imagined; prayer can and will lead to transformation of both ourselves and our world in ways we never envisioned. At its most basic, prayer can ground us in the essence of peace and freedom. All of this is possible if, and only if, we can begin to enter into prayer in a manner that has ancient roots but is new to many of us. And this way is through the path of the mystical, the place where prayer can come alive in the most powerful of ways.

I will readily admit that it is difficult to let go of traditional prayer, especially of the petitionary kind. It certainly was hard for me to give up this transactional brand of praying. It is ingrained in us from our earliest memories of childhood. We pray for things to happen. We pray that God will intervene and change our circumstances. It's very natural. Intercessory prayer is especially powerful at the bedside of a loved one who is severely ill and in pain. Who doesn't find great comfort in praying to God to restore a person to health, to end their suffering and bring them back to us for at least a while longer? This gives us hope, and hope is something we desperately need in those times. Praying for healing is as natural as lemonade in the summer! It's just what we do.

I will admit, even as I have begun to shift my prayer life to the more mystical and contemplative, I still find myself at times embracing the mantle of theism by praying for something. I feel really strange and kind of guilty when I do it, yet I do fall back into previous ways of being when it comes to prayer. But I know that I am not alone. The great theologian Marcus Borg, who has opened the doors to Progressive Christianity for millions of Christians, wrote this on his experience of prayer:

> *I do not think of God as interventionist, that God decides to answer some prayers. To imagine that God sometimes intervenes leaves all the non-interventions inexplicable. And yet, I do both petitionary and intercessory prayer. I pray for help for myself. I also pray for health, and help and protection for family, friends and the world. Doing so is a natural expression of caring. For me, it would be unnatural not to do this. And not to do so because I can't imagine how it works would be an act of intellectual arrogance. So I don't believe that God sometimes intervenes to answer prayer. But*

this doesn't prevent me from thinking that prayer sometimes has effects, even though I can't imagine how. I am very willing to think of other ways of imagining God's relation to the world, such as speaking of divine intention and divine interaction. At the very least, I am convinced that prayer changes us, that it transforms those who pray. This has been my experience.[46]

I resonate deeply with what Marcus Borg is saying, and I have a feeling that many of you, even the most theologically progressive, do as well.

As part of my research for this sermon on prayer, I Googled some of the great mystics to get a grasp on what they had to say about prayer. I love their thoughts on meditation and prayer, with a focus on stillness, love and connection with humanity. A short time later I checked my Facebook page, which not coincidentally served up a related post called "A Three Week Course for Pastors on Prayer." Out of curiosity I clicked on the post, and the page I was taken to said something like this: "This sermon series is designed for Pastors to use for their midweek/weekend church services. Instead of coming up with sermons from scratch, save time and use this series to teach your church about prayer." Needless to say, I was hooked! So I entered my email address, and went and got my free three-week series on prayer, all written and ready to go. Just open the box and preach!

And yes, my friends, it was as awful as I am guessing most of you are thinking. Prayer was described here as talking to your friend Jesus. Prayer was explained to be a necessary pathway for you to change your outcomes in life (*I could work with this one!*). Prayer was to heal you and your loved ones from illness, or it was to atone for the taint of Original Sin that you reek of. Prayer was to appease an angry God. I could go on and on as did these awful sermons that are being preached from this canned garbage in all sorts of churches led by Pastors using this material. But I think you get the point.

---

[46] Marcus Borg: Eight Selected Columns from the Washington Post. "Prayer Transforms Us." *http://wesleyknox.com/images/BorgWashPost8.pdf.*

Let me just say that, while reading that stuff on prayer made my skin crawl, I am glad I went to the trouble to review it, because it reminded me just how out of touch many Christian churches are with current reality and why Progressive Christianity is so important. It also reminded me of that line again from theologian Karl Rahner, that "the Christian of the future will be a mystic or he (or she) will not exist at all", and that our traditional ways of being spiritual are passing away.

These prefab prayer sermons symbolize why so many people are walking away from religion in general, because it just does not align with what we know of the world, and maybe more importantly, that it just isn't meaningful anymore. We will either rediscover the mystical side to spirituality, or we will walk away gradually as a culture and as evolving people, and nowhere is this more clearly seen than in the area of prayer. The white-bearded guy in the sky changing things and being our friend is no longer a viable option. It's time we retire that fantasy for good.

I chose our two readings today because they speak of the power of connecting with this mystery we name God through prayer in a way that is ancient, yet unfamiliar to most of us today. In the story of Elijah, we hear of his cries, his pain, his longings as he lies down to die, but then we see that it is not until he experiences the sound of total silence that he is able to leave the cave and stand and face what he experienced as God. God was not in the craziness, the busyness, or the chaos of earthquakes, fire and wind, we are told. God was not there in the noise and powerful things happening around him. But in the sheer silence, he heard; this mystery we call God was most powerfully manifested.

When Elijah experienced total quiet, we are told, "he wrapped his face in a mantle, and went and stood at the entrance of the cave" and felt God in a whole new way of which he had never dreamed. Perhaps he experienced the depth of prayer for the first time, beyond the lure of words and power. It's a great story and metaphor for both the mystery we name God and how we connect with that mystery in prayer.

We could have also used the Psalms, which speak of seeking and connecting to God not in words and events and intercessions, nor in theistic ways as we call them, but in complete stillness and moments of emptiness. Psalm 46 comes to mind, where amidst all of the chaos, the Psalmist stops and says "Be Still, and Know God." The mystics have also been telling us this for a long time: "Nothing in all of creation is so like God as stillness," said Meister Eckhart. He also wrote, "The most powerful prayer, one well-nigh omnipotent, and the worthiest work of all is the outcome of a quiet mind. The more silent it is the more powerful, the worthier, the deeper, the more telling and more perfect the prayer is. To the quiet mind all things are possible. What is the quiet mind? A quiet mind is one which nothing weighs on, nothing worries, which, free from ties and from all self-seeking, is wholly merged into the will of God and dead to its own." And let's not forget about these words he wrote: "If the only prayer you ever said was 'thank you,' that would be enough."

We could go on with thought after thought from the world's great mystics on prayer as a contemplative experience, a communing with God in the stillness and silence. There is such fertile ground here, for in this kind of stillness and quiet, prayer becomes fully alive and the heart of God is truly discovered and experienced most intimately and powerfully. That's ultimately the purpose of prayer, and the mystics and others who were able to transcend the limits of their religious traditions sensed this long ago. The time has come for us to join them and see prayer in a whole new way.

This is really what I want to say on prayer, and perhaps what differentiates our sermon from the canned garbage available online for one low price. The fact is that prayer is not about forgiveness, though you may feel the experience of forgiveness by engaging in it. Prayer is not about talking to your friend Jesus, though prayer can help you to see the Jesus Way in clearer and more powerful terms and that can strengthen you to walk that path with peace and courage. Nor is prayer about healing your loved ones, though you may feel great hope in focusing your energy, your life force, on someone's behalf, your own behalf or on behalf of the world in which you live and move and share your being with others.

There is no right or perfect way to pray, regardless of what people tell you. Prayer, if it is engaged in mystically and consistently, in times of quiet and stillness, in good times and not-so-good times, it will transform you and it will change your heart. This is true whether you pray through *meditation*, the art of stillness and silence; or through *centering prayer*, the art of choosing a sacred word or image and returning to it when you feel your mind getting busy; through *Lectio Divina*, the art of sacred listening to something that seems scriptural to you; or through *breath prayer*, the art of focusing on your breathing as the breath of the universe. Any and all of these are ways of connecting to the mystery we call God within and around you in wonderful ways. Prayer is about all of these.

It is also about deep listening to the world around you, especially nature; prayer is about gazing at the cosmos in awe and wonder; prayer is about time spent with a friend or loved one and just enjoying one another's company; it's about engaging your body, such as in yoga or tai chi, or just walking outside and opening yourself up to reverence for the earth and interconnection with all its diversity and wonder. Prayer can even be about working for justice. Feeding the hungry is a deep act of prayer and connection.

My point is that prayer does not happen only when you need something, and it does not happen only with your head bowed and your hands clasped, and it does not happen only on Sunday mornings. There is so much power and beauty in prayer, if we can just let go of the paradigm that tries to tell us otherwise, and as Gibran said in our second reading, "begin to expand ourselves into the living ether". Fewer words, more stillness; fewer thoughts, more quiet; fewer worries, more peace. That's the prayerful life, and it's a great way to live. Amen.

20

Study Groups and other Ideas

Sermons are not the only means of introducing the new doctrinal information of the last two hundred years. In this chapter we will mention several other avenues or approaches that may be taken. None of them are extraordinary. Use them if they fit your situation.

Study Groups

Sunday school classes are, of course, a form of study group, and a natural opportunity for imparting information, if already in place. In cases where classes do not exist, consider forming such a group for the express purpose of introducing new and challenging discussions. A book study is an expedient way to start. Here are a few suggested books:

> *A New Christianity for a New World*, Bishop John Shelby Spong. Bishop Spong calls Christians into a new and radical reformation for a new age. Spong looks beyond traditional boundaries to open new avenues and a new vocabulary into the Holy, proposing a Christianity premised upon justice, love, and the rise of a new humanity—a vision of the power that might be. (Description from Amazon Website.)

Putting Away Childish Things, Marcus Borg. Borg uses his core teachings on faith and the Bible to demonstrate their transformative power and potential in Putting Away Childish Things: the moving, inspirational story of a college professor, her students, and a crisis of faith. (Description from Amazon Website.)

Why Christianity Must Change or Die, Bishop John Shelby Spong. Bishop Spong integrates his often controversial stands on the Bible, Jesus, theism, and morality into an intelligible creed that speaks to today's thinking Christian. In this compelling and heartfelt book, he sounds a rousing call for a Christianity based on critical thought rather than blind faith, on love rather than judgment, and that focuses on life more than religion. (Description from Amazon Website.)

The Dishonest Church, The Rev. Dr. Jack Good. An unblinking look at the reasons behind the decline of the mainline churches, and a prescription for a long overdue remedy: honesty! It is also a celebration of a faith tradition that continues to evolve as it confronts the Ultimate Mystery. The book insists that the only way to preserve this tradition is to allow it to do what it has always done: adjust to new realities. Readers will be affirmed in their desire to stand at the intersection of a dynamic tradition and an open future. (From book cover.)

With or Without God, Gretta Vosper. Rev. Vosper addresses the issues of spiritual fulfillment, comfort and connection in the modern world through a thoughtful and passionate discourse. Offering difficult but penetrating insights into a new generation of spiritually aware—and spiritually open—people, *With or Without God* offers a startling model for a renewed church as a leader in ethics, fostering relationships, meaning and values that are solidly rooted in our own selves. (Description from Amazon Website.)

Misquoting Jesus, Bart D. Ehrman.When world-class biblical scholar Bart Ehrman first began to study the texts of the Bible in their original languages he was startled to discover the multitude of mistakes and intentional alterations that had been made by earlier translators. In Misquoting Jesus, Ehrman tells the story behind the mistakes and changes that ancient scribes made to the New Testament and shows the great impact they had upon the Bible we use today. He frames his account with personal reflections on how his study of the Greek manuscripts made him abandon his once ultraconservative views of the Bible. (Description from Amazon Website.)

What's the Least I Can Believe and Still Be a Christian?, Rev. Martin Thielen. Pastor and author Martin Thielen has compiled a list of ten things people need to believe, and ten things they don't, in order to be a Christian. This lively and engaging book will be a help to seekers as well as a comfort to believers who may find themselves questioning some of the assumptions they grew up with. With an accessible, storytelling style that's grounded in solid biblical scholarship, Thielen shows how Christians don't need to believe that sinners will be "left behind" to burn in hell or that it's heresy to believe in evolution. And while we must always take the Bible seriously, we don't always have to take it literally. (Description from Amazon Website.)

The Great Spiritual Migration, Brian McLaren. McLaren, a leading voice in contemporary religion, argues that—notwithstanding the dire headlines about the demise of faith and drop in church attendance—Christian faith is not dying. Rather, it is embarking on a once-in-an-era spiritual shift. For millions, the journey has already begun. (Description from Amazon Website.)

Re-Claiming the Bible for a Non-Religious World, Bishop John Shelby Spong. Bishop Spong argues that 200 years of biblical scholarship has been withheld from lay Christians. In this brilliant follow-up to Spong's previous books Eternal Life and Jesus for the Non-Religious, Spong not only reveals the crucial truths that have long been kept hidden from the public eye, but also explores what the history of the Bible can teach us about reading its stories today and living our lives for tomorrow. (Description from Amazon Website.)

The Future of Faith, Harvey Cox. Harvard religion scholar Harvey Cox's landmark exploration of why Christian dogmatism is giving way to a grassroots Christianity rooted in social justice and spirituality. Cox laid the groundwork for modern religious writing with his 1965 classic, The Secular City, paving the way for writers like Diana Butler Bass, Karen Armstrong, Stephen Prothero, and Deepak Chopra, who calls The Future of Faith "a fresh vision for the resurrection of a new global Christianity." (Description from Amazon Website.)

There are many other books available that provide entry points for introducing Biblical scholarship. Many are listed in the bibliography of this book.

Feedback Sessions

Feedback or talkback sessions—discussed in more detail in chapter 19—when held following the worship service, provide the laity with an immediate opportunity to express their views, or ask questions regarding the subject matter of the sermon. Such a session is quite important following a progressive sermon to allow for clarification of information, answering questions, etc. Pastors who hold feedback sessions on a regular basis will have no problem with the process. Those who have not tried this means of communication with their parishioners may feel uneasy at first, but as the laity warms to the idea of open and frank conversation about religious matters, a great deal of education can take place.

Special Presentations

Presentations in the form of videos and DVDs are readily available and are great teaching tools. Listed below are several for your consideration.

> *Painting the Stars: Science, Religion and an Evolving Faith*, by Living the Questions (Seven sessions) Available from *ProgressiveChristianity.org*. This video series explores the promise of evolutionary Christian spirituality. Featuring over a dozen leading theologians and progressive thinkers, the seven-session program includes a downloadable/printable participant reader written by evolutionary theologian Bruce Sanguin, and a facilitator guide with discussion questions. The basic format for each 1- to 1-1/2 hour session includes conversation around the readings, a 20-minute video presentation and guided discussion. (Description from Progressive Christianity Website)

DreamThinkBeDo -Young Adult Education, by Living the Questions (Twenty sessions) Available from *ProgressiveChristianity.org*. Looking for a springboard to get young adults talking about what Christianity is all about for this generation? DreamThinkBeDo is an engaging catalyst for conversation among young adults searching for what's next for followers of Jesus. Starting with the foundation of "Love God with all your heart, soul, strength, and mind," (Luke 10.27), DTBD is what Christian educators have been looking for to help college groups build a 21st Century faith. (Description from Progressive Christianity Website)

Saving Jesus Redux, by Living the Questions (Twelve sessions) Available from *Livingthequestions.com*. A total revision of Living the Question's popular 12-session DVD-based small group exploration of a credible Jesus for the third millennium. (Description from Living the Questions Website)

How Jesus Became God, Professor Bart Ehrman. (Three sessions). Available on YouTube, Part one opens at; *https://www.youtube.com/watch?v=7IPAKsGbqcg*. Parts two and three are listed on the sidebar.

Misquoting Jesus in the Bible, Professor Bart D. Ehrman. (One session, 1hr 39min). Available on YouTube at; *https://www.youtube.com/watch?v=pfheSAcCsrE*

How the Bible Explains Suffering, Professor Bart Ehrman. (One session, 58min). Available on YouTube at; *https://www.youtube.com/watch?v=y7cmUCjnCgE*

Why Christianity as We Know It is Dying, Bishop John

Shelby Spong. (One session, 36min). Available on YouTube at; *https://www.youtube.com/watch?v=Pcaw8XWiB-A*

Burke Lecture: The Terrible Text of the Bible, Bishop John Shelby Spong. (One session 1hr 23min). Available on YouTube at; *https://www.youtube.com/watch?v=yZM3FX1L Mug*

Several video lectures, Bishop John Shelby Spong. (Various lengths). Available at; *https:// johnshelbyspong.com/videos/*

Liturgy

The information/knowledge put forth in this book has an impact on the words we use throughout the worship service—preaching, teaching, singing, praying. For those who would seriously move toward a more intellectually honest Christianity, it will be necessary at some point to begin to adjust the liturgy of the Sunday service. Helpful hints for doing this can be found on the Progressive Christianity.org website in the section called Gathering Planning, a library of liturgical resources. This project contains resources for every element of the service, every season of the year, every age, every text, and more. Find it at *https:// progressivechristianity.org/worship-planning/*

Educational Presentation

The information found in Chapter 17—The Synoptic Gospels, lends itself to being a standalone presentation for a congregational gathering. It can be presented in one ninety minute session or three shorter sessions (one for each gospel).

These are but a few ideas for those who wish to introduce an honest Christian doctrine to their constituents. Additional ideas and resources will be found as one begins to explore those above and becomes more involved in the Progressive movement.

21

A Final Word

Whether you believe what you have read in this book, or not, is entirely up to you. Either way, you are a winner. Why? Because, as the renowned newscaster Paul Harvey would say, "Now you know...the *rest* of the story!"

Not only do you know the popular understanding of the Christian faith which you have been taught since childhood, you have now been exposed to the world's most scholarly understanding of the Christian doctrine, an understanding that follows two hundred plus years of critical examination of the Bible and Hebrew/Roman history, along with the scientific knowledge of the twenty-first century.

You have probably never heard a pastor refer to the Easter story as metaphorical. Nor is it likely you have ever heard her or him refer to the God of the Bible as a human construct of the ancient world. But such things are well known to biblical scholars, and are widely taught in mainline Christian colleges and seminaries. They are also fairly common knowledge to the younger, more educated members of our society, who find the Church and much of its traditional dogma out of touch, irrelevant, and unnecessary.

Whether you believe this information or not is a personal decision. But if you choose to dismiss it, we would suggest you ask yourself this question; "Where did *my* knowledge on these subjects come from that would make it more relevant than that of the world's leading Christian scholars?" If you give serious consideration to this question you may conclude, as many do, that your Christian education started somewhere around the third grade Sunday School level and hasn't progressed much since. You may have continued to attend Sunday School through your teens and even into adulthood, but if you look closely at the lesson plans of each of these levels of study, you will find that they are, most likely, patterned after the same two-thousand-year-old dogma you were taught as a child. And in a great many cases, you will find that the messages in those lessons imply a literal interpretation of the scriptures.

Unless Christianity can find a way to advance the knowledge of those who profess the Christian faith today so that that faith again becomes relevant in a more educated society, the likelihood of a continued decline in the number of churches and church members is a foregone conclusion. It is not an impossible task—re-education. There is still a window of opportunity, but that window is closing fast. We must find a way to become more educated about our faith, or stand by as the Church continues to self-destruct.

We have tried to help in this educational process by publishing this book. But it is only a small start; much more must be done. You can be a part of the educational process by sharing your copy of this book or suggesting that others acquire their own copy. You might consider starting a small study group in your church or in your home, using this book or one of those suggested in Chapter 20.

It is time for Christians everywhere to become active on our own behalf, if we are honestly concerned about the future of the Church. No one else can do it for us; we are the Church of today, and if we simply plan to leave the heavy work to the next generation, we are, for all practical purposes, giving up. There may *be* no church of tomorrow.

Certainly no one can predict the future with complete and perfect accuracy, but we contend that there remains an important place in society for Christianity and the Church—in whatever form it may take in years to come. However, the viability of the Christian faith can only be sustained if we who are the Church today care enough to question many of the ancient beliefs that no longer work in the modern world. Our beloved Church must become more intellectually honest if it is to survive in the twenty-first century. This is our challenge:

> *Job One - Advance the knowledge level of those of us who are the Christian faithful to a truer and more honest understanding of ancient Christian doctrine; one that reflects the true historical and scientific world view of the twenty-first century.*

> *Job Two - de-emphasize what one "believes", orthodoxy; and emphasize how one lives, orthopraxy (i.e. living the teachings of Jesus).*

We hope you will join us in embracing this new, exciting and *honest* Christian paradigm !

Notes

[1] Allen, Grant, *The Evolution of the Idea of God*, Escondido, CA: The Book Tree, 2000

[2] Good, Rev. Jack, *The Dishonest Church*, Haworth, NJ: St. Johann Press, 2008

[3] Graves, Kersey, *The World's Sixteen Crucified Saviors*, New York, NY: Cosimo, Inc, 2007

[4] Pew Survey, "Many Americans Uneasy With Mix of Religion and Politics," No pages, Online: *http://pewforum.org/politics-and-elections/many-americans-uneasy-with-mix-of-religion-and-politics.aspx#4*

[5] Battle, John A., "Charles Hodge, Inspiration, Textual Criticism, and the Princeton Doctrine of Scripture, "*The Christian Observer*, No pages, Online: *http://christianobserver.org/charles-hodge-inspiration-textual-criticism-and-the-princeton-doctrine-of-scripture/*.

[6] Study of the Therapeutic Effects of Intercessory Prayer (STEP), No pages, Online: *https://www.ncbi.nlm.nih.gov/pubmed/16569567*

[7] Bracken, Joseph A., *What are They Saying About the Trinity?*, New York, NY: Paulist, 1979

[8] LaCugna, C. M., "*Trinity*", Encyclopedia of Religion, Vol. 14, pg. 9360, Farmington Hills, MI: Macmillan, 2005

[9] Driana, C., *"Holy Trinity"*, New Catholic Encyclopedia, 2nd ed. Vol. 14, 201, Farmington Hills, MI: Gale, 2003

[10] Fortman, Edmund J., *The Triune God*, Eugene, OR: Wipf and Stock, 1999

[11] Encyclopedia Britannica, *Trinity*, Vol. 11, 928

[12] Lohse, Bernhard, *A Short History of Christian Doctrine*, Minneapolis MN: Fortress, 1966

[13] Dennett and LaScola, *Evolutionary Psychology*, Online: *https://ase.tufts.edu/cogstud/dennett/papers/Preachers_who_are_not_believers.*

pdf

[14] Allen, Grant, *The Evolution of the Idea of God*, Escondido, CA: The Book Tree, 2000

[15] Barnes, Harry E., *An Intellectual and Cultural History of the Western World*, 3rd rev. ed. Vol. 1, New York, NY: Dover, 1965

[16] Freud Sigmund, *The Future of an Illusion*, New York, NY: W. W. Norton, 1961

[17] Spong, John Shelby, *Re-Claiming the Bible for a Non-Religious World*, New York, NY: Harper One, 2011

[18] Public Religion Research Institute, No pages, Online: *http://www.prri.org/topic/religion-culture*

[19] Ray, Roger, *Progressive Faith and Practice*, Eugene, OR: Wipf and Stock Publishers, 2014

[20] Online sources, Churchleadership.org: *http://www.churchleadership.org/apps/articles/default.asp?articleid=42346/*, Pew Forum *http://www.pewforum.org/2015/05/12/americas-changing-religious-landscape/*, CNN.com: *http://www.cnn.com/2015/05/12/living/pew-religion-study/index.html*

[21] Plumer, Fred, Progressivechristianity.org. *https://www.youtube.com/watch?v=FBiOA0euuYU*

[22] Wikipedia, *https://en.wikipedia.org/wiki/Progressive_Christianity*

[23] Jones, Paul and Kea, Perry, *A Progressive Jesus for Progressive Religion*, *https://www. westarinstitute.org/upcoming-events-calendar/minneapolis-2016/*

[24] Wikipedia, Progressive_Christianity *https://en.wikipedia.org/wiki/Progressive_Christianity*

[25] Pewforum.org, *http://www.pewforum.org/2015/05/12/americas-changing-religious-landscape/*

[26] Borg, Marcus, *The Heart of Christianity*, New York, NY: Harper One, 2003

[27] Tillich, Paul, *Systematic Theology Volume One*, , Chicago, IL: The University of Chicago Press, 1951

[28] All quotes from scripture were taken from the New Revised Standard Version translation, 1989

[29] Ray, Roger, *Progressive Faith and Practice*, Eugene, OR: Wipf & Stock,

2014

[30] Campbell, Joseph, *The Power of Myth, With Bill Moyers*, New York, NY: Anchor Books Doubleday, 1988

[31] _____Ibid, 56-57

[32] _____Ibid, 261

[33] For more information, see *www.pewresearch.org*, A Closer Look at America's Rapidly Growing Religious Nones, May 13, 2015.

[34] Campbell, Joseph, *The Power of Myth, With Bill Moyers*, New York, NY: Anchor Books Doubleday, 1988

[35] Fox, Matthew, Meister Eckhart, *www.newworldlibrary.com.*, Letting Go, July 17th, 2014.

[36] *http://www.guinnessbookofworld'srecords.com*

[37] Barth, Karl, *The Word of God and the Word of Man*, New York, NY: Harper & Brothers, 1957

[38] Ehrman, Bart, *Misquoting Jesus*, New York, NY: Harper Collins, 2005

[39] Borg, Marcus, *The Heart of Christianity*, New York, NY: Harper One, 2003

[40] *https://www.youtube.com/watch?v=zHFDepyaJqo*

[41] Armstrong, Karen, *A History of God*, New York, NY: Random House 1993

[42] _____ Ibid

[43] _____ Ibid

[44] Borg, Marcus, *Meeting Jesus Again for the First Time*, New York, NY: Harper Collins, 1995

[45] Fallon, Mike, *The Real Face of Jesus*, Popular Mechanics, January 23, 2015. *http://www.popularmechanics.com/science/health/a234/1282186/*

Bibliography

Adler, Mortimer. *Truth in Religion.* New York: Macmillan, 1990

Allen, Grant. *The Evolution of the Idea of God.* Escondido, CA: The Book
   Tree, 2000

Allport, Gordon. *The Individual and His Religion.* New York: Macmillan,
   1950

Armstrong, Karen. *A History of God.* New York: Ballantine, 1993

———. *In the Beginning.* New York: Alfred A. Knopf, 1996

Barnes, Harry E. *An Intellectual and Cultural History of the Western World.*
   3rd rev. ed. Vol. 1-3. New York: Dover 1965

Bass, Diana Butler. *Christianity for the Rest of Us.* New York:
   HarperCollins 2006

Benson, Andrew. *The Origins of Christianity and the Bible.* Clovis, CA:
   Prudential, 1997

Blood, Barry. *Christian Dogma.* Xulon, 2004

———. *Giving Voice to the silent Pulpit.* Wipf and Stock, 2011

Borg, Marcus J. *God in 2000.* Harrisburg: Morehouse, 2000

———. *The God We Never Knew.* San Francisco: HarperSanFrancisco,
   1998

———. *The Heart of Christianity.* San Francisco: HarperSanFrancisco,
   2003

Bowker, John. *God : A Brief History.* New York: DK, 2002

Bracken, Joseph A. *What are They Saying About the Trinity?.* New York:
   Paulist, 1979

Cox, Harvey. *Religion in the Secular City.* New York: Simon and Schuster,
   1984

———. *The Future of Faith.* New York: HarperOne, 2009

Crossan, John Dominic. *The Historical Jesus*. New York: HarperCollins, 1992

Cupitt, Don. *After God*. New York: BasicBooks, 1997
———. *Reforming Christianity*. Santa Rosa, CA: Polebridge, 2001

Doane, Thomas. *Bible Myths and there Parallels in Other Religions*. Amazon Digital Services, 2011

Draina, C. 'Holy Trinity.' *New Catholic Encyclopedia*, 2nd ed. vol. 14, Farmington Hills: Gale,2003

Ehrman, Bart. *God's Problem*. New York: HarperOne, 2008
———. *Jesus, Interrupted*. New York: HarperOne, 2009.
———.*Misquoting Jesus*. San Francisco: HarperSanFrancisco, 2005.

Frazer, James G. *The Golden Bough*. New York: Avenel Books, 1981.

Freud, Sigmund. *The Future of an Illusion*. New York: W. W. Norton, 1961

Friedman, Richard E. *Who Wrote the Bible*. New York: HarperCollins, 1989

Funk, Robert W. *Honest to Jesus*. San Francisco: HarperSanFrancisco, 1996

Geering, Lloyd. *Christianity Without God*. Santa Rosa: Polebridge, 2002

Good, Jack. *The Dishonest Church*. Haworth, NJ: St. Johann, 2008

Goff, Vernon G. *Making God Talk Make Sense*. Lincoln, NE: Dageforde, 2001

Graves, Kersey. *The World's Sixteen Crucified Saviors*. New York: Cosimo, 2007

Greenberg, Gary. *101 Myths of the Bible*. Naperville, IL: Sourcebooks, 2002

Fortman, Edmund J. *The Triune God*. Eugene: Wipf and Stock, 1999

Hadden, Jeffrey. *Religion in Radical Transition*. Chicago: Aldine, 1971

Halloway, Richard. *Doubts and Loves*. Edinburgh: Canongate, 2001
———. *Godless Morality*. Edinburgh: Canongate, 1999

Helms, Randel. *Who Wrote the Gospels*. Altadena, CA: Millenium Press, 1996

Hood, Bruce M. *Supersense*. San Francisco: HarperCollins, 2009

Hopfe, Lewis M. *Religions of the World*. New York: Macmillan, 1987

Keck, Leander E. *A Future for the Historical Jesus.* Nashville: Abingdon, 1971

LaCugna, C. M. *'Trinity.'* Encyclopedia of Religion, Vol. 14, Farmington Hills, MI: Macmillan, 2005

Laughlin, Paul Alan. *Remedial Christianity.* Santa Rosa: Polebridge, 2000

Lohse, Bernhard. *A Short History of Christian Doctrine.* Minneapolis: Fortress, 1966

Magee, Dr Michael D. *The Hidden Jesus.* United Kingdom: Ask Why!, 1997

Mead, Loren B. *Five Challenges for the Once and Future Church,* Herndon, VA: Alban Institute, 1996

Olsen, David T. *The American Church in Crisis.* Grand Rapids, MI: Zondervan, 2008.

Overstreet. *The Mature Mind.* New York: Franklin Watts, 1959

Paine, Thomas. *The Age of Reason.* Amherst, NY: Prometheus, 1984

Pelikan, Jaroslav. *Jesus Through the Centuries.* Binghamton, NY: Yale University, 1985

Ranke-Heinemann, Uta. *Putting Away Childish Things.* New York: HarperCollins, 1995

Robinson, John A. T. *Honest to God.* Philadelphia: Westminster, 1963
————. *The Human Face of God.* Philadelphia: Westminster, 1973

Russell, Bertrand. *Human Society in Ethics and Politics.* New York: Routledge, 1992

Spong, John Shelby. *A New Christianity for a New World.* HarperSanFrancisco, 2001
————. *Eternal Life: A New Vision.* New York: HarperCollins, 2009
————. *Jesus for the Non Religious.* San Francisco: HarperSanFrancisco, 2007
————. *Reclaiming the Bible for a Non-Religious World.* HarperCollins, 2011
————. *Rescuing the Bible from Fundamentalism.* HarperSanFrancisco, 1992
————. *Why Christianity Must Change or Die.* HarperSanFrancisco, 1999

Stenger, Victor J. *God, The failed Hypothesis.* Amherst: Prometheus, 2007

Taussig, Hal. *A New Spiritual Home.* Santa Rosa, CA: Polebridge, 2006

Tillich, Paul. *Systematic Theology.* Vol. 1, Chicago: University of Chicago, 1973

—. *The Shacking of the Foundations.* New York: C. Scribner's Sons, 1948

Unknown. 'Trinity.' Encyclopedia Britannica, Vol. 11, Chicago: Britannica, 2005

Walsch, Neale Donald. *What God Wants.* New York: Atria, 2005

Wright, Robert. *The Evolution of God.* New York: Back Bay, 2010

Made in the USA
Columbia, SC
04 March 2018